Detroit City Poetry 2001

ABANDON AUTOMOBILE

Detroit City Poetry 2001

ABANDON AUTOMOBILE

EDITED BY MELBA JOYCE BOYD AND M. L. LIEBLER

WAYNE STATE UNIVERSITY PRESS   DETROIT

Library of Congress Cataloging-in-Publication Data

Abandon automobile : Detroit city poetry 2001 / edited by Melba Joyce Boyd and
M. L. Liebler.

    p. cm.

    ISBN 0-8143-2973-X (cloth : alk. paper) — ISBN 0-8143-2810-5 (pbk. : alk. paper)

    1. American poetry—Michigan—Detroit. 2. Detroit (Mich.)—Poetry. I. Boyd,
Melba Joyce. II. Liebler, M. L.

PS572.D45 A28 2001

811'.6080977434—dc21   2001002028

"The New World," "Photography 2," and "Salt and Oil" from *The Mercy: Poems* by
Philip Levine, copyright © 1999 by Philip Levine. Used by permission of Alfred
A. Knopf, a division of Random House, Inc.

"Three Journeys" from *Wild Gratitude* by Edward Hirsch, copyright © 1985 by
Edward Hirsch. Used by permission of Alfred A. Knopf, a division of Random
House, Inc.

For other acknowledgments, please see Contributors and Credits, beginning on
p. 403.

Homage to Frank O'Hara:
Why I am not a New York Poet

Detroit

Ken Mikolowski

CONTENTS

Abandon Automobile: Detroit City Poetry 2001 is as contrary as its title. This collection of poetry is distinct in its contrariness, in poets nurtured in the vitality and complexity of a city bound to the grit and bravado of urban struggle. With language born with that same tenacity, they are wedded to the beauty of literature and the excitement of words craftily configured on paper to interpret their world.

Their imagery is a mixture of artistic ascension and working-class clarity. They are more often than not the offspring of factory families and the legacy of labor unions. At the same time, Wayne State University, the hub of educational and literary activity, provides an informed, creative center for Detroit poets. To a large extent, they represent the most educated working class in the United States, adapting the literary to the fundamental funk of rock and roll or free verse reinvigorated with jazz rhythms and riffs. Their imagery converges with the cross fire of conflict and uncertainty like the Detroit River flowing along the coast of its Motown blues. These printed voices, heightened by the intensity of Latino salsa and the sticky sweetness of baklava, pull out all the stops to find the skyline they recognize.

Detroit poets cling to the craziness of resistance in the face of literary traditions, and they scoff at the rules of conventional politics. Despite the conservative shift of society, Detroit poets are melded and embellished by diversity. They delve into unknown depths and garner creative energy as ideology. The tongues that speak on these pages belong to a city that made its reputation as the Promised Land, a point on the North Star, away from lynching and blood-red Alabama clay. Detroit was the harbor in the Great Lakes, a place to dock beyond the dim light of Lady Liberty, away from centuries of European poverty. It was the possibility on the other side of the Mexican border, a direction away from picking dusty crops.

The poets of this time and place recover the dead streets of a once vital Paradise Valley. They remember and give voice to ghosts living underneath newly paved streets, deadened by hollow corridors and dreams deprived of passion. From the vanquished magic of Spanish accents that linger in the aftermath of confrontations with American English, poets save and savor the grace of ancient, indigenous sensibility. From the unseen strength of Slavic undertones, poets inhabit corners of vigilant neighborhoods. Contesting the onslaught of natural and unnatural storms, they invent new visions and open an old life to an earth renewed.

It is in the poetry that Israel and Islam greet in a language seeking a victory larger than God's special blessing. It's in the poetry, in the jazz of its vocabulary, in the black invisible of the white, in the moonlight of the darkest distance. It is in the poetry, where the humanity of the city meets without compromise.

These poets speak with a fluidity of identity. They encode cultural relationships in the in-between space of foreign countries, along the borderlines of previous nations. They bridge neighborhoods with words that touch the flush of colors and that taste the salt and wine of everyday doings and beings.

Detroit poets write about the city as a living entity: it is a cocoon, warm and familiar; or a beast that awakens in the dead of night to haunt a wonderland where disturbances, perversions, and resurrections occur without note or notice. Poets mark the buildings, name the streets, count the corners, recall the stench of factory fumes. They embrace the memory of romance and the disappointment of another revolution gone awry. The blood vessels of these poems pulsate without apology and often with unusual tenderness and resolution that make fragments appear whole.

These poets listen to the hum of history and the clash of metal. They reveal life still striving in the refuge civilization forgets, but never forgives. They meld poems from the rust of abandoned automobiles, detecting the molecules of disfigured flesh grasping at hidden shadows for promises, reconfiguring the triangles of shattered glass, freezing the mirror staring back at them. They write under the shade of weathered trees, bathe their words in a river that withstands the undertow of the Great Lakes, and with each new poem rebuild meaning for the city.

Melba Joyce Boyd

The title of this collection of poetry, *Abandon Automobile: Detroit City Poetry 2001*, was adapted from a sculpture by poet Ibn Pori Pitts, which illustrates this cover. From the frame of the abandoned automobile, Pitts created an art piece that illuminates themes found throughout this anthology. The colors, lines, and language refracted on the hood of this Buick attempt to retrieve the discarded, identify the abandoned, and bring forth beauty found in distinct places and in unique expressions. For us, the static adjective "abandoned" was translated into the dynamic verb "abandon," a transformative act that posits this poetry as having visionary insight.

In assembling an anthology of poems from and about Detroit, we had to consider the unique diversity of Detroit's population. Our aim was to create a collection that verbalizes a century of eclectic, historical patterns — layers of language in configurations of reds, blues, greens, yellows, whites, browns, and blacks — that present a literary collage grounded in Detroit's demographic. The poets appearing in this anthology all have significant ties to the Detroit area: whether as native sons or daughters, current residents, or temporary residents during a crucial stage in their creative development. Their poems were selected because together they reveal the city's sensibility, its consciousness, and its unbridled vitality.

The unique contribution of Detroit poetry to American literature is as distinct as the city's historical contribution to the Industrial

Revolution. Before Henry Ford induced thousands to work in his factories for five dollars a day, Detroit was largely regarded as a port city set on the border between the United States and Canada. This geographical factor made the city one of the last stops on the Underground Railroad for runaways from southern slavery. Today, African Americans make up 83 percent of a population also comprised of Western Europeans, Greeks, Italians, Slavs, Latinos, Arab Americans, Asian Americans, and Native Americans. The city's economic decline in the last decades of the twentieth century, due to a shift from an industrial-based economy to a technological one, has drastically altered the circumstances of the working class. These past and present socioeconomic configurations have affected the development of Detroit's literary community and are reflected in the imagery of its poetry.

In the 1940s, 1950s, and 1960s, when Detroit was the "Arsenal of Democracy" and the "Automobile Capital of the World," industrial wealth embellished the city's educational and cultural institutions. In tandem with the city's industrial identity, poets emerged from a myriad of ethnicities. Literary relationships of historic note, such as the friendship between Dudley Randall (1914–2000) and Robert Hayden (1913–1980), demonstrated how the automobile industry and the labor struggle stimulated artistic expression and aesthetic exchange in the working-class and the African American community.

During the Great Depression in 1937, Randall and Hayden met and provided aesthetic sustenance for each other and their artistic pursuits. By day, Randall labored in the Ford foundry, while Hayden worked for the WPA. By night, Randall and Hayden met at the YMCA to discuss literary techniques and their own writings. In fact, Randall typed Hayden's first manuscript, *Heart-Shape in the Dust*, for submission to a poetry contest. Although it did not win the prize, Falcon Press, founded by a group of union organizers, published the manuscript. Randall and Hayden struggled to be published in national magazines because of the limited outlets and opportunities for black poets.

The poetry community grew as emerging educational programs provided intellectual and creative space for these new artists. Wayne State University played a major role in this evolving literary movement. Many of the writers included in this anthology have either studied, worked, taught, or read poetry at this university. Wayne State is located in the heart of the city's cultural center, alongside the main branch of the Detroit Pubic Library, the Detroit Institute of Arts, the Detroit Science Center, Your Heritage House, the Children's Museum, the Detroit Historical Museum, the Charles H. Wright Museum of African American History, and the Center for Creative Studies.

The more senior poets, Philip Levine, Henrietta Epstein, Dudley Randall, and Murray Jackson were students at Wayne in the post World War II era. Some were students in the Department of English and were members of the newly formed Miles Modern Poetry Workshop, directed by Professor Chester Cable. Some of their earliest poems were analyzed on campus and published in issues of *Milestones*. The Miles Poetry Series hosted poetry readings by local and nationally renowned poets. The Department of English at Wayne provided the formal training for many Detroit poets, many of whom were factory workers or the sons and daughters of factory workers. They crafted images and institutions that became instrumental to the cultural industry of the city.

Wayne State University also became a catalyst for poetry activity in convergent and progressive ways. When Rosie E. Poole, the Dutch scholar, was a visiting professor at Wayne, she took a particular interest in Detroit poetry. In 1962 she published *Beyond the Blues*, an anthology of black poetry, in the Netherlands because she could not find an American publishing house that would accept a poetry manuscript by black writers. That same year, Margaret Danner, a Chicago writer and poet-in-residence at Wayne, founded Boone House. Boone House held poetry gatherings and readings for black poets in Detroit such as Naomi Long Madgett, Oliver LaGrone (1906–1995), and Dudley Randall. In 1968 five black and five white writers formed a workshop, and published an anthology titled *Ten: An Anthology of Detroit Poets*.

Dudley Randall was a member of Boone House when he composed "Ballad of Birmingham," following the 1963 Ku Klux Klan bombing of the Sixteenth Street Baptist Church in Birmingham, Alabama for *Correspondence Magazine* in Detroit. In 1965 folksinger Jerry Moore asked for permission to record the poem as a song. In order to protect his rights as the author, Randall printed the poem as a broadside, a single sheet of paper, and founded the Broadside Press. Shortly thereafter, he began the *Broadside Series* and published poems by such prominent black poets as Robert Hayden, Margaret Walker, Naomi Long Madgett, Gwendolyn Brooks, LeRoi Jones (Amiri Baraka), Melvin Tolson, Jean Toomer, and Langston Hughes. He called the first set of poems "Poems of the Negro Revolt." As the press grew, it began to publish books by these same broadside authors, and it also introduced new black voices of the 1960s, including Don L. Lee (Haki Madhubuti), Etheridge Knight, James Emanuel, Nikki Giovanni, Sonia Sanchez, and Audre Lorde. According to poet and scholar Eugene Redmond, Broadside Press became "the hub of black poetry publishing."

Under Randall's auspices, Broadside also published emerging Detroit-based poets: Jill Witherspoon Boyer, who was also the editor of the Broadside Annual; Melba Joyce Boyd, who was Randall's assistant editor (1972–77); Aneb Kgositile, who served as an editor for the press (1977–80); John Sinclair; and Michelle Gibbs. Broadside Press was the most successful small poetry press at the time. More than five hundred thousand books were distributed between 1965–77. It served as inspiration for other aspiring, small presses.

Randall's colleague Naomi Long Madgett founded Lotus Press in 1972. Its first publication was Madgett's *Pink Ladies in the Afternoon*. Like Randall, Madgett realized that only through independent presses could black poets ensure that their works would be made public. She extended her resources and skills to other poets and published the works of noted Detroit poets Toi Derricotte, Paulette Childress, and Bill Harris. Since 1972 the press has grown significantly, claiming 76 titles.

The racial dynamics of the times influenced and characterized the city's ever-growing poetry community. Broadside Press was an outgrowth of the Civil Rights Movement and was energized by the Black Arts Movement. Likewise, the antiwar movement and women's movement radicalized other sectors of the literary world. Many Detroit organizations and venues surrounding the Wayne State University campus became addresses for historic poetry readings and workshops advancing a counterculture that articulated a working-class perspective and an activist vocabulary.

In 1964 poets and musicians founded the legendary Artists Workshop (1964–67) on Forest Avenue near Wayne State University. Poets Robin Eicheles, John Semark, John Sinclair, George Tysh, and Jerry Younkins and musicians John Dana, Charles Moore, Ron English, and Lyman Woodard created a vortex for a unique mix of avant-garde poetry and experimental music, which captured the cultural scene. Like the names of their poetry publications, *Change* and *Work*, this new workshop believed that consciousness of one's art was as provocative as jazz/poetry readings and performances. The Workshop recorded music, published city poets, and brought in national names for the billboard such as Allen Ginsberg, Ed Sanders, and Robert Creeley.

The Artists Workshop was the stimulus for starting the Alternative Press in 1969. Editors Ken and Ann Mikolowski created a press that gave national opportunity for Detroit-based poets Jim Gustafson, Mick Vranich, John Sinclair, Donna Brooks, Faye Kicknosway, Chris Tysh, and George Tysh. Like Broadside Press, the Alternative Press extended its identity beyond city borders by publishing noted national poets Robert Creeley, Allen Ginsberg, Anne Waldman, Gary Snyder, and others. Their publishing format was as varied as Randall's press, which included broadsides, postcards, and bumper stickers. The goal of the Alternative Press was to create an eclectic, accessible, and inclusive mix of writing for audiences, and an alternative community for artists.

During this plethora of activity, there was limited interaction between the racially segregated literary communities, even though there was some collaboration between individuals. Poet and publisher Dan Georgakas explains in "Young Detroit Radical, 1955–1965" how the cross-fertilization of radical politics and culture in Detroit resulted in collaborative publishing projects during the 1960s:

> There was a strong self-publishing movement among Black writers in the city, as Black writers were then virtually excluded from literary anthologies of major publishing houses. Dudley Randall began the influential Broadside Press in the 1960s. His press and mine had one joint venture, a wall poster by M. B. Tolson. This kind of interaction between the Black artistic community and radicals was considerable but totally unstructured (URGENT *Tasks* 12 [summer 1981]).

It was during the 1970s, as the city began its dramatic economic decline, that small presses and reading series began to showcase a more diverse roster and encourage more cross-cultural activity within the broader poetry community. The number of independent presses also increased: Wayne State professor and poet Steven Tudor founded the One Hundred Pound Press; Glenn Mannisto, Dennis Teichman, Chris Tysh, George Tysh, and Jim Wanless founded the Detroit River Press, and Mannisto edited the newsletter *Straits*; and in 1973 Carl Aniel, Greg Hallock, Jeffrey Ensroth, Larry Wilson, Sharon Vanden Brock and M. L. Liebler started the Ridgeway Press and the Rideway Artist Collective, which was influenced by surrealism, Dada and the Fluxus Movement.

The most profound change occurred in 1980, with the establishment of *Lines: New Writing Series* at the Detroit Institute of Arts. For the first time, the Detroit poetry community experienced cross-cultural artistic exchanges on a consistent institutional basis. George Tysh, the director, established workshops for veteran poets, beginning writers, and children. Tysh also structured the poetry reading series by pairing Michigan poets with out-of-state poets. Some of the featured out-of-state poets were William Burroughs, Robert Duncan, Margaret Atwood, Kathy Acker, Amiri Baraka, Quincy Troupe, Ntozake Shange, Jayne Cortez, Alice Walker, Lorenzo Thomas, Jim Carroll, Pedro Pietri, John Cage, Jessica Hagedorn, and many others. As director of

Lines, George Tysh's most important overture was building a collective poetry community, one that dramatically altered the direction of Detroit poetry and publishing. Most of the poetry reading series and publishing activities became inclusive and collective. For example, in collaboration with Broadside Press 1983, Detroit River Press published *Song for Maya* (1983) by Melba Joyce Boyd, illustrated by José Garza. Likewise, John Sinclair began a poetry, jazz, and visual arts program at the Detroit Council of the Arts that combined the full tapestry of the city's artistic and ethnic expressions. In addition to his museum program, Tysh also aired poetry on Wayne State University's public radio station WDET-FM. *Dimensions*, a poetry program, was hosted by Tysh, poets Dennis Teichman, and Glenn Mannisto. Sadiq Bey also hosted a poetry and jazz program for WDET during this same time.

The 1980s also saw the emergence of the *Metro Times*, which printed announcements and features on the readings at the *Lines Series* and poetry activity in the city. Concurrently, Sadiq Bey initiated the *City Arts Review* for the Detroit Council of the Arts, and in the Cass Corridor, Ron Allen established the *Horizons in Poetry* (H.I.P.), a multicultural poetry series that resulted in the publication of a representative anthology of Detroit poetry. Wayne State University's Annual Colloquium Poetry Series also began at this time. Poetry readings at Alvin's, a local pub, were the talk of the day, and any poet worth his or her rhythm read there at least once. New magazines, such as Kofi Natambu's *Solid Ground; New World Writing* brought attention to writers like Sharazetta Natalege and Leslie Reese. Joan Gartland founded the feminist, cultural journal *Moving Out*. Thom Jurek and Pat Smith's *Southpaw* and Chris and George Tysh's *In Camera* appeared. Christine Monhollen, Dorinda DeLiso, and Mary Taylor edited *Triage: New Writing*, a unique journal of art and poetry, featuring the visual art of Sherry Hendricks. Sherry Hendricks also published her visual art and writing in *Detroit 1981, Detroit 1982*, and *Detroit 1989*. Dennis Teichman and Debra King established Past Tents Press, which had the most ethnically and artistically diverse roster: Mick Vranish, Bill Harris, Melba Joyce Boyd, Kofi Natambu, Chris Tysh, George Tysh, Dennis Teichman, Kim Hunter, and Ken Mikolowski.

When Henrietta Epstein became the director of the Poetry Resource Center (PRC) in 1980, the office moved from western Michigan to Detroit. The PRC hosted an annual poetry festival, poetry and fiction readings, literary talks, and seminars, and published a monthly newsletter, *Rock 'N' Read Marathons*. It also held a large collection of Michigan literary books in its in-house library. However, in 1991 severe cuts in funding for the arts on the state and national level brought about the PRC's demise. The Detroit Council of the Arts was also sorely affected by conservative policies related to arts funding.

Despite funding setbacks, poetry in the city during the last decade has benefited from an increasing number of poets at Wayne State University and the perseverance of independent poetry presses in the community. The Detroit chapter of the YMCA National Writer's Voice Project, directed by M. L. Liebler, services readings, workshops and performances for Detroit poets and poets from the across the country. It has grown into one of the largest literary centers in the country, connecting poets and introducing poetry to the general public. This includes the annual UAW-YMCA Workers-Writers Festival, Poetry at the Opera House, The Vision of Words Non-Traditional Venues Workshops in domestic abuse shelters, youth homes, and prisons, local YMCA after-school programs, the Detroit Festival for the Arts, and the Detroit Literary Festival.

In the 1990s poetry slams, performance poetry, and rap poetry gained popularity. Open-mic readings at coffeehouses and bars are now a common characteristic of Detroit's nightlife. Broadside Press continues to host the Broadside Theatre founded by Randall in 1980, and to publish new works. Similarly, poetry as the printed word has been preserved by the diligence and impressive productions of Detroit independent presses founded in the 1960s, 1970s, and 1980s, which maintain national and international reputations.

When Mayor Coleman A. Young named Dudley Randall the first poet laureate of Detroit in 1981, he applauded Randall's leadership as a poet and publisher of poetry. Randall's achievements are exemplary, and yet they are reflective of the Detroit poetry community as a whole.

Similarly, the recent naming of Naomi Long Madgett as poet laureate of Detroit reiterates the value of the poet/publishing tradition. Most of the poets in this anthology are artisans as well as artists. They nurture and till the cultural terrain with style.

The poetry in this collection is largely the consequence of cultural investment in the creative consciousness of a troubled city. These poets are closely tied to the music and the matter of urban struggle. As Detroit moves into its fourth century, its poetry will continue to be the vocabulary of creation and of resilience, insisting on telling it like it is, to "abandon automobile."

Detroit City Poetry 2001

ABANDON AUTOMOBILE

Sarah Addae

Sunstruck

The city has moved too close to the sun
this July,
Last night, laying in bed,
nine months pregnant and wondering,
lights flickered across the dark rooms,
and when I rose to look,
there were great mountains of Sun
in the night sky.
The store on the corner was transformed by fire.
I crawled through the attic window, onto the porch roof,
watching mobs of sparks take the darkness, take the electric wires,
take the coolness from the air, and with their heat,
drive me inside.

Today, I was painting the bathroom fern-green,
in celebration of new life,
while the trees tapped at the window outside.
Through the filter of the leaves
huge orange flowers
leapt into bloom.
I stepped onto the front porch, into the heat,
and saw the house next door,
long since abandoned,
encased by fire.

With empty lots between us, I stared at the halo of flames.
The summer heat made waves,
the fire exploded upward,
the sun glared down among it all.
With no one else on the street,
All I can do is say a little prayer;
"Icarus, come down now,
Icarus, please, come down."

Saladin Ahmed

Stereo Links

On my way to the store
Strange links boom out of Cadillac windows
Stereotypical dichotomies collide in my gut
Old World vs. New World
East vs. West
Jihad vs. G.I. Joe
An amalgam of continental contradictions
placing the midnight blue clay of Phoenicia
into the industrial blast furnace of Detroit
Its end product?
Ani
Me
The accidental occidental

Strange links boom out of Cadillac windows:
"You dropped a bomb on me, baby!"
Cousin Khadija moved in with us
'cuz the Israelis really had dropped a bomb on her

Audio vibrations from the
youth of my youth
drown me in childhood:

Jidu, grandfather, in his little garden,
wrinkled brown
hands pulling up parsley

Occasionally, decades of unfiltered
Camels and Ford plant smoke
would bring up an unearthly hacking cough
that would seemingly transform Jidu
from a Lebanese elder
into the Baptist preacher I'd seen
when visiting church
with my best friend Cornell:
    "Salah-Al-Din, go to store . . . MmmHAGH!
    buy beans, rice . . . . MmmHAGH!
    we have *mjudara* for dinner . . . MmmHAGH! . . . HAGH!"
In childish confusion, I'd respond
the way Cornell's mother would:
    "Tell 'em Jidu!, Tell 'em ALL about it!"

Back to present day, old age of my youth returns
as the vertigo of cultural juxtaposition recedes.
All-too-familiar links boom out of
Lincoln Town car windows:
    "Reports today indicate . . . blah blah blah . . .
    continued fighting . . . blah blah blah . . .
    Islamic fundamentalists . . . blah blah blah . . .
    Terrorist activity . . . blah blah blah!"

Wishing these links were strange, I continue
on my way to the store.

Incinerator

You can't dial 1-800-NO-BREATH
to save you
from toy box
Coleman's box
You can't dial 1-800-NO-BREATH
to save you.
All the lines are busy.
No one's at home to issue new
air.

Hey! How bout a poly chlorinated
dibenzo p-dioxyns cigarette?

There is no "NO BREATHING" section
on this flight.

Gotta suck Coleman's world through
a Hydrogen chloride straw.

Coleman's toy box has the malicious
mechanized motion of lead.

It has split the saltpeter tongue with dioxyns
of biochemical air zones of putrid
organisms.

It emits unmitigated insufferable
if unchallenged chromium fists
stuck in the malleable throats
of an innocent breath.

Come on! Coleman's scabrous fingers
the greedy digits of grief
play with the dry pussy of sulfur
dioxide the new colonial bologna
in your chemical sandwich.
In our face
In yo face
In our absence of face.

Hydrogen chloride this baby of hell
won't no water put this fire out.

We're one breath away from choking on
this titty of volatile organic compound.

Death don't suck away this smoke
of stench stolid polysyllabic compounds
that eradicate life.

There are some bad mother fuckers baby
those are some bad mother fuckers.

You can't dial 1-800-NO-BREATH
1-800-NO-LUNGS
1-800-NO-FACE
1-800-NO-HAIR
1-800-NO-DICK
1-800-NO-LIFE
1-800-NO-WOMB

All the lines are busy
being chewed by nitrogen oxides
and arsenic.

And no one's home to issue

new air.

The Phraseology of a Mood

for Donald Gaines

the moon is raw light
swallowing whole my scream
i am the nite squad
of the lifeless needle
my teeth chewing the brittle dark
my veins are stuck in the gutters
that gargle the blood of its victims
i eat from the empty bowl of god
there is no music
to distort my eye or
correct my vision
i grow from the soil like snakes
weaving amongst the breath of plants
i am looking for symbols
& i am left with words
i look inside them
for their rhythm to seduce
them with the wine of my ideas
ra speaks through my form
it is him u see
mirrored in my gaze

my guts are angel hair
they form webs
i live in this cocoon
nothing is to come
my fingers grasp the nothingness
to squeeze from it meaning
to push through my lips and speak
as i eat from the empty bowl of god

Trumbull Song

Once a girl were
from land of Trumbull
and tree named streets
but more than
the name
the place she flies above
at night and in dream

she see the field
on corner
once a house
were right there
Sam the Tailor
locked up
Sharky's dark
pay phone hanging
the apartment
on Butternut
all its bricks stolen
and no roof

she go over
the store now
Norm's Liquor
Express
she see a deer there

in the parking lot
smelling garbage
the air

across the street
the church
gargoyled and black
like fire
once just touched
parts of its outside
like the deer were
too had escaped
from another place
time to breathe again
and run fast
or fly above
like on a carpet
knees tucked underneath

but tomorrow
in the daylight
when she rides by
the deer is gone
she stares there
from the window
and wishes it safe
back in a field
or a forest

because it is the names
that might fool you
Pine, Sycamore, Spruce
Elm, Ash
and the stillness
of almost daylight

that could
get you lost
make you crazy
fly in circles
like garbage
or slow like
a tumbleweed
down deserted
Trumbull Ave
and she above it
can see it
fix it all up
in her dream
from the air

it is the stillness
she takes with her
when daytime does come
and the distance
is different
from the ground
she remembers
all her nights
and is calm

as she walks now
home from school
streets and blocks
she finds a picture
in her mind
of every different tree
shape of leaves
and she wants
the deer back
to walk with her

these now bright
tree lined streets.

For D. M.

She was an expert on the color blue
remembers hands, seashells,
dresses, flowers, swings
from the grass beyond the school
staring at the building
she notices light
in a way we only
wish we could touch.

They could draw you a story
write every day down
birds' nests and closets
they went into and never left
gunshots and fires and car accidents
and days in the park made of only old
tires smelling rubber and smoke
because sometimes it is like
the city never does stop burning.

But some things still stand
have to when it is the place
you call home
lots of other people too
laughing and waiting for busses
getting haircuts
and riding up and down that hill
on Bagley like it might
never end.

In a city where friends
become old train stations
strong birds reoccupying
overgrown fields
where do you fit in
somewhere near these things
and a bridge like a backdrop
waiting for that time
when all its lights come up.

I am glad you are there
in an empty classroom after school
thinking good thoughts
like birds and baseball and
soon it will be my birthday.

And for today the smoke
in the fifth-floor window
on the southwest side
of Michigan Central Depot
is only a cake tucked in a corner
of the room
waiting for you.

Motoring

Just once more,
I'd like to take a ride in my father's car,
the way we did when we were small.
"Let's go for a drive," he'd say,
never liking movies or TV.
We went "adventuring"
on the East side, the mysterious Orient
of small tool & die factories,
remote auto-maker's mansions,
the blue-grey expanse of St. Claire,
and the Pointes,
their perfect greenery, noiseless streets,
and quaint, inviolate shops
like replicas of shops—too nice
for customers.

Sometimes, we'd head down
toward the hub, navigating
the old neighborhoods,
bunched, dense with brick porches
and double balconies,
remains of trolley tracks beneath our wheels
bumping us towards gothic spires,
Girly Shows, and neon bars
with living rooms above.
He coasted us under the giant billboard-man

who blew real smoke rings in the air,
and by hundreds of narrow windows
with tan shades half-drawn
like hooded eyes.

as he pointed out, there
and there, how it used to be,
and how it's all changed since,
raising, with a lift of his chin,
the frames of places,
from thirty years before: The Cream
of Michigan, the hangouts
of the Purple Gang, The Gaiety Burlesque—
rocking us in our cradle car,
past the ghostly Greystone Ballroom
into a palimpsest of parables and times.

One rainy afternoon, he slid us up
to a sly stop, and,
without warning, made a knowing cut,
into a turn-of-the-century
cul-de-sac,
strange park of huge despondent lawns,
and desolate cupolas,
turrets, gables, domes, wrought-
iron gates and fences,
and an empty carriage house.
Slowly, he went round and round,
and round again and then
he brought us back, and on we went,
into the trafficked roads of other vistas,
other worlds, lived or living
in the deft maneuvers of his pilot hands.

Olivia V. Ambrogio

They Say God Marks

picture
2 grey-brown flurries of
spring passion spinning on the street
in their own whirlwind
imagine such frenzied
joy, the heart in each
wing
beat
a racing pulse of desire too strong
to notice an approaching roar
of cold metal and thick fumes impervious
to the balmy air

Only at the last minute
do 2 quick shapes dart as Cupid's arrows
from the ground
only at the last does one swoop back
in exuberant arc to be
cut cruelly off midair
by steel tons:
a half-turn,
and premature descent.

Picture
beneath the dissipating smog

from a small bundle
of feathered twigs
a weak flutter
like a prayer

Alvin Aubert

You'd Have to See It

our brown bomber
as metonymic bronze
forearm in tripodic
suspension

as truncated bronze
fist-headed arrow aimed
battering ram straight
straight at the heart of hart plaza

on the river front in downtown detroit
bereft of his legendary brawn
tripodic stance.

The Numbers

even the lady who serves me breakfast
at the corner soul food place does it
by the numbers. like in ledbelly's waking up blues
numbers be all in the grits, folded in with the scrambled eggs.
the waitress yells back into the kitchen her regrets
she didn't play the numbers she dreamt
that turned out to be the winning combination
the day before, beginning with the first three digits

on her shiney new michigan license plate.

"i used to play 'em regular," she says, "seems i hardly
play 'em at all anymore, since my first husband
died and my second husband not caring for me to."

numbers in and out people's lives like squirrels
tumbling from trees in the cross hairs of a seasoned hunter.
her second husband's a seasoned hunter who dreams
of squirrels dangling by the teeth from the nape of his neck,
clawing at the zipper on his pants, going straight in for the kill.

Chene Park

One old fellow contemplating others

does it matter their ages vary,
that they're hardly ever all
in one place together? in the eyes
of one are the vacuousnesses
of them all, wherever in the world
they are. they're here, in chene park

they're everywhere and all at once
under the sun and in the softer
silences of the moon. the stars
in their rambling constellations
seen by one are seen by all
holding their fortunes tightly in their reigns
in a jumble of signs noticeably unzodiacal.

it so happens one is a poet
far past being invited anywhere,

too timid to crash anybody's party.
an old versifier in a tattered coat
who once broke down and cried
before a sizeable audience
while reading one of his poems—

how else should he be remembered
but as the senescent versifier of sorts
beyond redemption who unabashedly
cried while reading one of his poems
before an embarrassedly captive audience?

Irvine Barat

Four Decades Ago

It's a neighborhood
you're glad you don't live in
tired bars
hang-around types
with chronically thin wallets
girl-women who parade their emptiness
on a faded street
peddling the only product they own
and those who crowd the files
of caseworkers

Crossing the Detroit River in the year '54
in a personal war of independence
I squatted in an unappetizing flat
of aging walls
made tolerable by the colour of posters
and handed over sixty dollars a month
to a bedraggled landlady
for two dingy rooms atop creaky linoleum steps

But that was yesterday
before software and e-mail
when other men were bald and the grass was green

Today I return to breathe forty years of indifference

stores and apartment buildings have suffered neglect
no social worker could condone

Chris and Carl's where I sipped 2 A.M. coffee
after bar closings
before trudging home
blighted—savaged
its pale brown stone front
marred by slum-boarded windows
decorative plastic cubes smashed

and the Chin Tiki that bragged
authentic Polynesian cuisine
tropical drinks
vainly proclaiming its former elegance
by a mosaic above the front door
of colourful Aztec design
a fifties' beauty queen
now a near-death crone

And the apartment building
where I dreamed and worried
boiled water in a pitted pot
fried 8A.M. eggs on a resale-shop stove
annihilated by a wrecking ball

Now—standing before a vacant lot
bounded by freeway and alley
a rectangle of mud that once was home
I muse
on the fragility of existence

Faruq Z. Bey

Kantos

A Chant for the Work of Tyree Guyton

Artist . . .
For lack of a better
In the Motown at the Millenium
He be seeking to draw
    To question "limits"
    In this mephistophilian order

The calling . . . the work
To superimpose
Hidden in bicycle seats and
Dismembered doll heads
These pillars, consonants
Over whimsical vowels
In an Indo-Aryan syntax

This calling . . . the work
Is it a class thing or a race thing
The calling . . . the work
Is it a class thing?

The neighbors whose aesthetics
Are drawn from light-speed glimpses
At the burbs who
Long to shoulder the harness

That will bring them into
The light of day
Garlanded with flowered epiphanies
Is it a class thing?

Splotches spires
And wandering circles
A hankering graffiti that
Threatens a world
That would know only sheer
Plane surfaces . . . would glisten
And commissioned diadems

A ghetto
        A found aesthetic
That spawned tone deaf virtuosi
Who died screaming in alleyways
Or slumped over spikes

Artwise
Is it a race thing?
Avantart artwise
In this sight
a poverty
This . . . a dearth of black bohemians
In this a dumbing down
A chorus of whispering shadows
A spasm in the search
        For image
                For meaning
A class thing

Lost . . . the color
Of reggae the taste
Of a song

Morning 85

during the ceremony, of course
she was late, swollen with admiration
and witnessing the genetic mass
thrown, barreling towards the future,
my child was not fair, "the memory-
frozen image," she wore makeup and
a long black weave to match the sexy
black dress . . . my child is an adult.
the realization so peculiar, it's easier
to accept a twenty-five year old woman,
holding gladiolas and taking pictures.
I must tell you, prayers are answered.

Terry Blackhawk

Reader Response

After teaching Yusef Komunyakaa's My Father's Love Letters
at Henry Ford High School, Detroit, Michigan

His discussion group has figured it out:
the mother did the right thing
by taking her leave, no matter the child
she left behind. But McMaine holds firm,
determined to see it his way.
When they point out how the line breaks
at "happy," the child "somehow . . . happy"
the mother had gone, McMaine reads
right past the happiness. The sentence ends
with "gone"—a stronger tone which to him
means forever. Dead. The mother in the poem
didn't simply excuse herself from bruises, abuse,
didn't become the dish that ran away
dodging the fist that would send her—
"Pow!"—to the moon. Not that tired story.
For him it's a deeper tale: bones buried
beneath a tree the small bird's warning
warbles from, a song so threaded
through his days, eyes, breath, mind
every tree he passes sings it, every mother's absence
means forever. Gone. The page blank.
The book closed. So when he leans to his paper
full of erasures and empty

of the details I would coax from him,
I think how what the mother serves the child
dishes out, creating always the same
painstaking pattern: the plate beside the knife
between the fork and spoon. I watch as he writes
"*What I remember about that day is*
(here he fills in a date) *my first birthday*
(in fact, his tenth) *without her*" —and I know I'm reading
an emptiness that has surely become
his polestar, his fixed center, a leaping beast,
an absence forever present in his sky.

February Teacher

Like Ariadne with her thread
I pass our grated storefronts. Hopeful shingles
—Tonsorial Parlor, Nubian Patios—
blur by. The burden is great this month,
the skies lower. Three stout women with mops
stand at the door of the Temple
of Deliverance, bend to the cold, pat
their pockets for a key.

I can't avoid this catalog of signs:
these cubistic messages leap out at me
from gritty angular surfaces. Salt,
dried in the asphalt, crackles underfoot.
Today we talked about Thoreau
treading his path to the pond,
and I know I mourn most
a loss of memory, how the buildings
sagged around this intersection, lock out
the impressionable earth.

I didn't do Henry justice today
but I was looking for you, and you'd driven on
with a laugh and a wave. It was last year
you ducked past me through the classroom door,
grinned and said, "I think I'm a transcendentalist."
I'd never take in all this architecture
at once, perpendicular planes, boarded windows,
but I think how you'd take this same roadway

and stretch it as far as you could, into a straightaway,
the Harley between your knees purring,
echoing your not-so-nascent energies, drawing you
away from our fumes into mint and leather
on the wind. You'd cross open pastures
and wade waist deep in the waters of the mind
and I'd send you on, tanked up, ready to go.
It's my job, you see, to rethread the maze, again
and again, never minding the scenery,
or lack of it, one-way streets, dead-ending.

The story always repeats itself. You survive
the labyrinth. Of course you leave me behind.
Midsummer nights will find me, beached, alone,
not regretting, as I look up, hear you roar away,
and the stars bend to join me.

Melba Joyce Boyd

We Want Our City Back

We want our city back.
We want our streetlights on.
We want our garbage gone.
We want our children
playing on playgrounds,
but not with loaded guns.
We want to retire
by the river
and raise collard greens
in abandoned fields.
We want our ancestors
to rest in peace.
We want our city back.

We don't want law and order.
We want justice and jobs.
We don't want small business.
We mean serious business.
No more Mom and Pop wig shops.
No more Mickey D's
rappin' with the homies.
No more Dixie Colonel
serving Kente cloth cuisine.
No more Taco supreme.
No more indigestion or

quick fix politics.
We want our city back.

We don't want police
harassing the homeless
for being without a lease.
We don't want video cops
busting crack heads
with flashlights at night.
We want peace keepers
to capture the real dope men
reclining in respectable privilege.
We want our taxes
to track down the real assassins.
We want our city back.

We don't want Euro-centric
or Afro-eccentric edu-macations.
We want a freedom curriculum.
We want a liberated vision
with history remembered.
We don't want our children crunched
like a computer chip
to fit
in the old world order,
worshipping slave holding
societies in Egypt or Greece.
We want the board of education
to take a lie detector test
for neglect of the intellect,
for assault on our children's senses.
We don't want them to be GM execs,
for rejects in labor camps.
We want dignity,

not cupidity.
We want our city back.

We want the river dragged
for distraught souls.
We want our homes rebuilt.
We want the guilty
to pay a greed tax
for the living they stole.
We want our city back.

We ain't going away
like fugitives escaping
to Canaday! Hey!
Our backs are up against the wall.
This is our clarion call!
Feed the hungry!
Clothe the ragged!
Heal the sick!
Enlighten the ignorant!
Punish the wicked!
And raise the Dead!

We want our streetlights on.
We want our garbage gone.
We want to be rid of smack and crack.
We want to retire
by the river.
We want our ancestors
to rest in peace.
We are claiming our history,
seizing the hour.
Cause, we mean to take
our city back.

● ◆ ●

the view of blue

the river
was what
they wanted.
they valued
the view
of blue—
a picture
in a window
with white lines
drawn by
mini
venetian
blinds.

the corporate state
measured and
maneuvered
the real estate.
they purchased
collusion
on the eve
of elections
in private rooms
where lawyers
convene with
judges,
the lords
of the discourse
of dismemberment.

they protected
the power
of wealth

and the right
of Americans
to shop for
that dream house
by the river
with the "Trail
of Tears" running
through it.

the undercurrents
of city corridors
dislodge and
disassemble,
by the law
of pre-eminent
domain.
the land was
remanded with
an eviction
notice.

the river
was what
they wanted.
they didn't care
how they got it,
or that
under the cover
of dusk,
rats run
the course
of the river
banks
and through
hidden alleys

to scour
plastic garbage
bags left
outside entrances
to servants'
quarters.

The Burial of a Building

On the occasion of the implosion of the J. L. Hudson's Department Store,
Downtown Detroit, October 24, 1998

when they bring
a building down,
when they make
history absent,
when they implode
a cistern of memories
into a basement grave,
where do
the ghosts go?

are they given
an eviction notice?
do they read
the headlines
of runaway newspapers
tumbling down
the street,
or do they
pass on
a posting
caught on a

jagged nail or
transfixed on
crumbling concrete?

did the ghost
of the light-skinned
"colored girl"
who ran elevator
number 5
call a meeting
between floors
to discuss
the demise?
or did the last
of the charmed,
posed mannequins,
hiding in the
bridal suite of
dressing rooms,
send out the
fatal alarm?

perhaps, one of the
under-employed,
excavating the remains
for bronze fixtures and
copper veins,
left an echo
in the alley
so disturbing
it alerted
returning souls—
disrupted their
eternal shopping
for imported

after-dinner mints,
for that exquisite dress
with the perfect fit,
for that pin-striped suit
for the anniversary
occasion, or for
another matching set
of muffs and hats
for Xmas past
celebrations.

did the ghosts follow our footprints
to sit atop our houses?
or did they hover next to
high-rise towers
and likewise, point
translucent fingers
and clink champagne glasses
filled with misty laughter?

or did the blast
call their skeletons
to attention,
disrupt such earth
bound musings
and with the wind
scatter them
with dust, ashes
and disoriented
pigeons.

another landmark gone—
another space left behind,
another hole in a story,
another burial

to collect bones,
another place
from where
ghosts
are gone.

Detroit Summers

down by the river
with winter coming on
greying the edges of the days
talk in the bar is slow
before he walks home alone
a little later.

summer was a fickle friend
or just helpless
against what an old man dreams—
it turned away.

again he says in the bar by the river
'50 was the best
someone else spits "48"
before he pushes up
to some paper-windowed room
to fill his years
with hot dogs and peanut butter—
not enough for a tired man
who has seen too many summers turn away.

Detroit City

thieves give more to blue
than hardness does
and where noon is
thirty floors of steel won't tell
now that time ticks
instead of filling spaces
and tenderness talks fast

thieves give more to dusk
than engines do
and what neon offers stars
makes beggars laugh
while birds stand by without applauding
the strangeness in the songs
that asphalt sings to trees

William Boyer

Squatter's Rights

January,
however frigid,
cannot cover
nor thaw
those concrete mounds, that glacial till,
steam-shoveled
into road marker burial grounds,
they signal your old neighborhood
like fish tails
poking through the sand
at the Belle Isle beach
Somewhere west of Atlantis
and south of Troy . . . .

Driving alone,
in circles,
I stalk the memories
which unclothed and fed us,
before we thought we knew better
the perfect metaphor for a city
besieged
by well-intentioned
self-destruction.

Yet these ghosts
are meant to be inhaled

and slept upon,
like the stolen hood ornament
(the closest I came to a ring),
or our rooftop blanket,
or my favorite t-shirt,
torn from leaping out
the two-story window
with your sister climbing up the stairs,
until the flashing midnight yield
blinks away the fortieth trance
and nostalgia slips back
into the ragweeds
and ghetto palms,
to rejoin the nonrefundable glass,
the plastic grocery bags
and the assorted housing materials
    we left behind.

Donna Brook

People Don't Die Just So You Can Write a Poem about Them

The night after Bradley shot himself
Ken and I started arguing about
how old he had been. "Bradley is,"
I said, "the same age as I am
or younger."

But of course there was as always
in these cases all that talent, a shoe,
Detroit, intelligence, orange, humor,
scarlet tongues and magenta crowd scenes
of goons and plumbing parts—

So, Bradley Jones, 1944—Till Yesterday,
now I am about to be
older than another dead person.

I Have My James Schuyler Too

Just because I lived in Detroit for 22 years doesn't make me
without memories or feelings and once John Ashbery
was in my charge when I was a graduate student, nobody
else was available to see he got lunch and from Macomb County

Community College to his evening reading, so it was just me
    and John
Ashbery eating in Warren, Michigan. He told me how
he had to have minor surgery and asked how much I thought
it would hurt and, of course, I only wanted
to hear what it was like to *know* Frank O'Hara.

All of today I've been wondering why I always thought
this particular woman you've probably never heard of
lives in Chelsea, and then tonight at the reading
for *The Diary of James Schuyler* at the Poetry Project,
in New York City, where I've now lived for 18 years.
I remember my son had said she lived on 23rd Street,
so, of course, I must have kept imagining the Chelsea Hotel,
the only reason I ever seem to think about 23rd Street,
just as James Schuyler is the only reason
I ever think about flowers.

In 1974 or so John Ashbery
walked in through my parents' front door
and out the back to their garage
so I could drive him to Wayne State University,
and the following Sunday my mother looked at a big picture
of him in *The New York Times Book Review* and said
to me with astonishment and almost a hint of accusation,
"This man walked through my kitchen!"

I suppose that's more or less
my mother's John Ashbery, and I have
my James Schuyler too.

Eastside Hypocrite

With grass in neat rows and
geraniums in level potting soil,
it nears 9 o'clock. Work people
are returning to their homes
as others abandon their families
for the night; leaving cashed stubs
and credit slips whisked under
handy linen piles.

An oblivious Chevette
sits in your driveway while
porchlights come on as they
did years ago. Little boys
still transform their bicycles
into horses and planes,
fast cars and spaceships;
while I sit on the same
porch and damn your dreams
of fame outside this Detroit.

Anthony Butts

Detroit, City of Straits

February finds a likeness of spring in this unicorn
embossed bedspread. Warm in its closeness, his palm

rests flat against his thigh. Downstairs, the chicken

is frying. The greasy smell wells up through the floorboards
of his small room, a kitchenette for a family cramped

into the upper-half of a one family house from the 30s.

The old stovepipe hole in the roof allows sleet
into a rubber bucket beside his bed

in the only room of the house without heat.

His breath rises on the loose clouds of winter blowing through rags
stuffed between a broken window and its screen.

He dresses quietly in the reservoir of dusk; the time is coming

to run errands for his father, to go looking for the younger brother
running in the streets with those girls from the neighborhood
   high school,

to go and buy a Bible with the money his mother

gave him, to look up those passages
that his pastor dunked him for last week.

The Belle Isle Men

Over by the horses,
    by the giant yellow slide,
the shoed but sockless
       men pace through the sundried dirt,
       through humid air lighting
on all those black legs
    sweating into the basins

of dress moccasins. Their mustaches
    are kept thin and close to the lip,
    close to the transplanted smiles
of Detroiters born in the Carolinas,
    of men who've learned to swallow everything.
The dusk blown into their eyes is the drought
    of women twisting in the shoreline silence,
    of cool evenings dying on the vines

of morning glories. The hum
    of lungs, of the larnyx, murmuring low
aren't calls from pens of happy animals
    or from the reclusive river skulking
    in the crevices of rocks.
Those murmurs are the revenge of lust
    exchanged like rage, like the world when viewed

from horizontal, the big scoop
    of sky turning over the soil
    as if the coming of day
would cover them.

Mary Ann Cameron

Hearing

can you hear the faint siss

tires of the ghostcars
on the rainy road

cars with sharp lines then
rounded streamlined cars
dark motorized buggies
and the small ghost rattle
of the streetcar

clopping hooves

the slight creak and clank
of the tack as a
furrow is plowed

can you hear the deer
can you hear trees growing
glaciers pass

can you hear the rocks
just being rocks a
million years before
anything else got here

I can barely hear the deer
the ghost deer

Haiku '84

    watching the tigers
beat the new york yankees: so
    who needs a love life

Smallness: Ann Mikolowski's Aris Koutroulis *(1985)*

City portrait
is tall and vast
as the Lord's Prayer written
on a grain of rice

Highland Park

alone, breathing deeply
looking about continually
slow stepping, hesitantly
Ghosts, watching ghosts,
abounded in the silence,
imposing their illusory will.
Unseen hands
tending unseen mills,
raised short neck hairs.
Three generations of ghost autoworkers
whispered, with hushed, groaning voices,
from dusty corners,
revealing billions of sweaty days
birthing millions of Tin Lizzys.
Proud Kahn columns, stalwart yet,
worthy of any Egyptian temple,
extended far beyond sight,
in perfect alignment.
Standing in a gutted restroom
amid broken bowls,
ankle deep in fallen Ford gray paint chips,
I could sense the perverse presence
of Star Men moving knees aside
to check
if there actually was

excrement in the bowl.
Small worn floor boards,
arrayed in the 1912 pattern,
bearer of countless work boot scuffs,
were missing, buckled, useless.
Ruined, wrecked cranes, rusting,
hulked abandoned, misted in fog,
showered by cold icy rain,
hundreds of feet
above black bays.
High bay,
alien in its antiquity, arched,
vaulted with blackened windows,
holy cathedral
of the ancient auto world,
faded softly, murmuring,
disappearing
into the mist.

Highland park, *mighty* Highland Park,
bombproof Highland Park,
likewise, into history.

Angelus Novus

After Edward Hirsch and Walter Benjamin

He saw police hauling away teenagers
carrying broken soda pop bottles
from Hart Plaza where the night before
dancers whirled at the Ethnic Festival.
He saw Fords and Chevys, the carcasses
of carmakers' assembly lines,
torched and overturned on the narrow lots
of warehouses stacked along the river;
the discount drug stores and gas stations
being looted, neon signs spreading their dust
over the ground like ashes of the dead,
and he saw onlookers hiding behind
newspaper boxes staving off the fury
of the exhausted crowd with a *Free Press*.
He was one of those bystanders who watched
the fires from the bus stop, waiting for
the transfer to Dearborn to go home from work,
and though the burning would finally calm
and disperse and drift, he understood
this night, which burst forth like a fever,
would last forever. He saw the storm of history
hurl the past onto the citizenry of Detroit,
piling wreckage upon wreckage, like
coal slags that rise above the horizon.

He kept his hands in his pockets,
his eyes fixed on the catastrophe, murmuring
about the storm blowing from Paradise,
propelling him into the future,
his back turned on the debris.

Jesus Turns Asphalt into Bread

> *Poetry is preparation for death.*
> Nadezhda Mandelstam

Interstate 94, at milepost 210,
I pull off heading to Henry Ford's
hometown. Ford-Addison Exit,
a stalled Chevrolet on the corner,
gray side-panel, its rusted muffler
fallen to the curb. Dandelions
and tall weeds in the alley,
the absence of irises. The point is
never to forget, to understand
every blessed day might last forever.
Past the traffic lights, another city,
Detroit in the rearview mirror,
blurring my vision a man as good
as any other I've never met
holds a sign that asks, "Why doesn't
Jesus turn asphalt into bread?"
He disappears, to the right, Chrysler
Glass Plant, an uncle's workplace
since early in the 1970s.
I know what I'm talking about.
"I work and I remember, that's all."
Lawrence Joseph understood this

conceivable language in New York
in 1982. Does it matter that each day
I pass St. Barbara's Elementary
where Sister Antoinette in the third
grade accused me of creating false
gods? I couldn't explain. The sky
absent, except for smoke that's drifted
eastward from the Rouge. Forget
the carmaker's words, examine
Coleman Young's: "Neighborhoods
collapsed because half the goddamn
population left!" I'd never forgive
the nun. I disciplined myself,
memorized the Quran's Opening,
studied the Sisters of the Nazarene
Catechism, cursed the factories
stretched out between Miller Road
and Fort Street. Monday afternoon,
security escalated near the United Nations,
Cubans in East Harlem argue whether
Fidel Castro will rent a room in their
borough. The temperature, cold.
I've been doing this my entire life.

Esperanza M. Cintron

Street Market Requiem

another new detroit poem

I came home to
a third-world street market
like dried fish in tin buckets
women with baskets on their heads
and brightly colored skirts
wrapped low, around their hips
void of civil-lie-zation,
department store marquees
and haute couture mannequins
there were, instead
riot gates and cardboard signs
letters dripping house paint
Koreans selling pock-marked goods
priced to steal
behind Plexiglas weeds
and long lines at the bus stops
the food stamp office and MESC
the streets reverting back
to pre-Model T days,
the aftermath of black reign
the penalty for post-colonial fervor
hemmed, rimmed in
by mall enshrouded suburbs
like the brick walls left by the French,

the Portuguese, the Belgians . . .
a circle of wagons
against poisoned arrows,
thrusting spears
and other strange habits
peculiar to survival.

I came home to
a third-world street market
the people, those "unfortunate vessels"
who had "cast down their buckets"
picked up spades,
watched over the sick, the dying
were the "best street sweepers"
had worked up to the foundry
now, displaying what is left of their wares
a little shoe leather, some heart,
a few are still breathing
no more colored elevator operators
hell, no more elevators
the Macon Deads and Luther Nedeeds
having securely double-knotted
their bootstraps
frequent high-priced stores
that sell kente cloth
to buppie leadened suburbia
done moved aside
ditching Castro's fourth world,
that oozing sore
to lay a red carpet
for gent-tri-fye-cation
for Archer's condos, Ilitch's stadium,
Pappas' casinos
selling out water rights

to cultivate a rippling Brooks' smile
for a chance, once again
to nurse somebody else's child
to till somebody else's soil.

Where Gardens Grow

Autumn skies cast their expressions crying, smiling and
touching the brows of men living with their isolation.
The trees give way to Nature's calendar, shedding orange and
red tears down on the wet concrete streets.
Old men dressed in heavy coats and hats pull their collar to
the winds watching the city go by too fast for their tastes.
Dark sooted busses roar by like urban dinosaur rat-catchers,
swallowing humanity and their mysteries so ancient God forgot
their reasons why.

Black kids rap-choir hold ground on nearby corner, dancing
in youth rituals where the beat is all, the rhymes of inner-
city disgust are spit at the sky.
Artists draw smiles on demon faces and send pictures of buried
treasure sailing out their windows to the poor folk below.
Gardens grow in cracks of broken empty parking lots where no-
body parked in years only the dance of mean old world blues
were heard walking and talking in the middle of the dream-
night.

Party time socially acceptable people gather to forget and to
remember at the various watering holes and secret rooms.
At Steve's Place for instance, old bluesmen sit and moan out
of tune stories of their youth and the crowd is happy.
One black gal moved by the emotional air stands up and sings
America the Beautiful; her gospel was spontaneous and grand.

Everyone applauds and she smiles, kisses her boyfriend and
they go back into their world of anonymous lovers.

The sun shines on odd days now illuminating the old peeling
paint on the sides of 1930s brick buildings. We see the
sights of black shades framing the faces driving their V-8
cruisers now 20 years old if a day. Roaring down Woodward
Avenue, past long gone diners and department stores left for
the dead and dreaming.
The sounds of busy downtown businesspeople leave at 5 P.M.
for suburban wasteland and fine-trimmed lawns full of hap-
piness and regret.
Just like inner-city and far reaching neighborhoods they
celebrate with caution and a desire to dream of a better life
somewhere else.

Parades happen here, hands hold babes still half asleep to
the hard-time news of what life is all about.
Billboards advertise technology to better the lives of us all
yet the skies still turn grey. The city reveals its caress
from time to time with a dim halo over its Motor City roof-
tops, but we still sing and pray.
You hear the bare trees carry the whispers and lies and
lovers' promises into the heaven of hearts undivided by mean
old world blues.
Such hard times we make for ourselves. Listen this cold
night, listen to the walls crumble before the all-faith gos-
pel of lonely explorers, lingering in the rooms of the once
Forgotten Individual.

Making history or living out the party days and nights of a
young soul searching, how we lived through self-devised hells
and almost mechanical recoveries from our mischief.
There we were and still are riding out the storms of growing
pains, working the assembly lines or cleaning the toilets of

rich bastard sons. You are forever reminded of your mortality and forever believing of the immortality of some inner faith you thought long since vanished.

Where the rusted metal fence post stops, the colors of rainbows are born from the ground up.
Flowers grow in abandoned houses where babes once cried.
Still we drive on solemn highways with no looking back.
Teaching ourselves to think on the streets of time. Never doubting that we all had a reason for being here one more day.

Andrei Codrescu

Detroit Love Song

*for my Detroit friends: the Incomparable Derelict Jim
Gustafson, the Impeccable Ken Mikolowski, the Joyful Ann
Mikolowski, the Wind-Hewn-Rock-Honest Mick Vranich, and
Roy "Flame-Keeper" Castlebury.*

Detroit gave me my first America.
19 years-old & scared I watched cars flow over John Lodge
    Expressway
and decided that they followed a law The Law of Cars
by which blue cars followed blue cars red cars red cars and so on—
I stood over the bridge there that cold March evening of 1966
    in my emigrant green thin nylon Romanian coat
    & shivered watching the car river
    wondering why I had come
    who I was
    was I always going to be this skinny
    was I ever going to get laid?

And at the Wayne State University cafeteria I tried talking with my
    hands
    to girls who mostly wouldn't talk to me
    and when they did I wrote
    in gratitude & abjection
lines of poetry on their arms and if they let me on their
    shoulders
& one or two let me write a poem all over them

& those were my happiest days
& those were my best poems
And on the second floor of that Wayne State University cafeteria
    that is no more
at the Lost & Found counter
    worked my future wife Alice
but I didn't know it yet
& walked instead relentlessly nervously walked
    without peace over the big boulevards and into strange
    neighborhoods
& past the burnt shells of factories
looking for the center of the city
wondering where the center of the city should be
    because I could not imagine a city without a center—
    that was inconceivable to me—
a center where everyone met, talked & maybe found love—
& when I asked people pointed me to shopping centers
    and malls and central offices
    & more shopping centers
& there was no sign of people meeting & talking in one place
    no sign of love—
& because my English was lousy I was always misunderstood
& when I said to the driver of the Dexter bus:
    "Can I buy this bus?"
    meaning "Can I ride it?"
    he shoved me rudely & said:
    "Go buy the Livernois bus!"
    & still no love
       & no center—
until the Trans-Love Energies commune on John Lodge!
A sign there said:
    "C'mon people love one another right now!"
& I went there & there was music & longhaired guys
    & girls mostly girls
    & they wore long skirts

& had big dreamy Sixties eyes that were just opening
wide out of the sleep of America
& that's how the psychedelic Sixties
came to Detroit & to me
& to the world Thank god
& the gray March drizzle turned party-colored
& I got rid of my emigrant green pitiful nylon coat
& let my hair grow and wore an amulet around my neck
& took LSD
which put me firmly & finally in the world
& allowed me to belong in it
& not only that
but one evening while in love with the world
& waiting for the bus
& having an odd powerful physical sensation that the planet
        even in Detroit
        kept surging unimpeded through plants & animals
    & things—
I saw a vision of beauty in the form of 2 girls coming toward
    me—
& I read to them from the book in my hand
    which was "Howl" by Allen Ginsberg
& they took me to hear the Muddy Waters Blues Band
    at the Chessmate Club
& one of those girls was Alice
    who worked at Lost & Found
    who had a big yellow bed
    in her tiny apartment on West Ferry
    & a typewriter
    & she found me I guess
    & then I wasn't so lost—
I started typing on her typewriter the poetry of that party-
    colored universe which strangely now
            even in Detroit
            pulsed stronger & stronger

& I called the book when I finished it a week later:
  "Insane People with Beautiful Sidewalks"
  for all the obvious reasons
& that was my first book in my new language & I was home.

Detroit gave me love & a center & music
  & a job at the Detroit Public Library
  where I rollerskated in search of books
  until one day I took some mescaline
  & rollerskated too long & too much & they fired me
  but that was OK
      because I knew a hundred people by then
          & we were all artists & writers & music-makers
& we wanted America out of Vietnam
& we wrote on the back of the Thinker by the Detroit Art
  Museum:
  WHAT'S THIS PIG
      THINKING ABOUT?
  THE TIME
      FOR REVOLUTION
          IS NOW!

And that was Detroit in 1966
  but by 1967 it was:
UP AGAINST THE WALL MOTHERFUCKER!
  & "C'mon Baby Light My Fire!"
    Jose Feliciano singing
& we turned around in the car to look
& downtown was in flames
    & then we had to lie on the floor
      of our artistic apartment
          full of collages & poetry
because there were tanks on Woodward Avenue
    & if they saw your head
      after curfew

they machine-gunned your building & killed you & everyone inside
    dead—
& that was Johnson's Great Society
& those tanks were elite U.S. troops
    from the 82nd & 101st Airborne Divisions—
& things weren't so much fun after that
& those who didn't die then
    wanted to leave
& those who stayed
    died anyway after that
with a few exceptions
I see happily here—

& that was it
except for a few million other things
& a handful of lifelong friends
with whom in the strangeness of faraway cities
    on various oceans
we practiced stories of Detroit
    —like an exotic rite—
& it's true
    in a way I was born here
        born an American here
        an American without a car
            in Motor city
                born in Detroit oddly enough
                    but never regretfully—

Rosedale Street

Rosedale (timeless, sometimes),
street of children,
village of dreams.
place of face
against wind, feet
against grass, sweet
pears and dragonflies.
here winter visions
become crystalline as snow
flowing across silver skies and thru coon capillaires.

this is a street of the wonderfolk.

Rosedale (timeless, sometimes),
street of yellow
sunflowers and turkey-time cornstalks.
what backyard farmer has planted
this thousand petaled lie? americana
anesthesia defines the old ones. ashanti
aesthetic, the young ones. music
and menthol cigarettes are the primary
intoxicants; alcohol, hemp, and crystals are secondary.
here bars and baptists nightly dance
to the tune of a ghetto's constant laugher/dirge.

this is a street of the wonderfolk.

Detroit Is in Renaissance

and the writers & the poets & the
musicians said there is in our fingers
tales to tell . . . what took you
they sd so long to arrive?

and the play(righters) &
the sleeping oil cans
made a pact with the publishing
house for canvas life
& the house let up signs that blinked
open for the business of births
& abortions whatever!

and the poets in ny sd most of
us schooled there in the 60s
& some in the 20s but no matter that
some of them was borned here
or made here once, like on a line
assembled, they was!

and the presses never stop
rolling & there is ink
filtering out into the streets
so much the paper is typing
that at lunchtime during rush hour
words of some poet have gotten

loose & *is* raising havoc
at Jefferson & Woodward, some
letters were found last week
in the scum at the bottom of
Belle Isle fountain & the City
promised to shut it down
until the perpetuators were
found and arraigned!

and the singers & the feet
sing the dance and dance the songs
that tell the passers-by
there be renaissance here. the passers-
by say, what? the passers-in say
what took you so long?

Robert Dana

Simple

In Memory of Stephen Tudor, 1933–1994, and
Lawrence Pike, 1932–1995

In the heat of the day
and a plague of house-
flies aboard. We're
barely moving on flat
water. The air, thick,
pressing. So Steve
sets the whisker pole,
and we wing-on-wing to
catch whatever breeze
there is. Not much.
Now, the waters seem
readable; the cries
of shore birds, speech;
a dragonfly, tethered
at the sheets, perfectly
still, a letter in some
Eastern alphabet aglitter
in the illiterate light.
But it's only we who doze
amid the sweet profanities
of language; the patient
spaces each word makes
to keep the day in place.

The only story told
will be the one we tell.
About how the temperature
drops suddenly, and the
north goes white; wind
like a hurricane's backspin
turning us a full three-
sixty, the tiller useless.
Larry looks like Neptune
in the stinging rain,
striking sail in the yaw
and pitch, shoving loose
gear below. The storm
jib steadies us now,
and the helm responds.
The rest of the story's
simple. No tricks. Hard
north. Well off the reef
above Grindstone City, run-
ning the troughs of twelve
foot curls, their dirty
crests breaking over
bow and gunwales. Three
hours later, our teeth
chattering with cold,
we surf home on long,
voluptuous rollers behind
Port Austin's breakwater.
The bar, My Brother's
Place, you'll love. Warm,
first flush of Daniel's;
the deep-dish pizza.
And you'll stay playing
pool, late into the night,
with the Ukrainian woman

and her two teenage
daughters. And she'll love
the look in your eyes
as you tell this story.

Jim Daniels

Hard Rock

You see, when you're a kid in a factory town, you got only two
choices—staying and enduring the factory life, or getting out.
But either way, you gotta be tough, you have to refuse to give
up. People in Detroit are faced with more pressure than kids
in other cities. There's got to be a release for the frustrations,
and Detroiters express that release through rock 'n roll.
Peter Wolf

A bunch of guys walk out
because it's over a hundred
and the bosses are passing out
pink salt tablets and saying
Get to work, like it's a normal day.

We stand around the parking lot
drinking beers. Spooner opens up his van
and puts his speakers on the roof,
booms out some kick-ass tunes. One by one
the guys take off their shirts
put down their beers and start boogying.

Somebody might say, Look at these guys —
if they can dance, they can work.
The plant manager standing by the gate
with a couple security guards
might be saying that right now.

He's the kind of guy who doesn't appreciate
good music. The kind of guy who'd say
This is not a pretty sight.
The sweat shines off beer guts,
dribbles down over tattoos, scars, medals,
flies through the air, everyone slick,
stomping their boots on the ground,
smelling tar, oil, and their own bodies,
their own bodies sweating because they want to,
and the crowd keeps getting bigger,
and we keep shouting
Louder, louder.

Detroit Hymns, Christmas Eve

Kenny and I down a few beers
circling church in my old Falcon
thinking about midnight mass.

White Castle is the closest we get,
sitting at the shiny metal counter
mumbling our little prayers.
Shoulda got a pint of something,
Kenny says.

Shoulda woulda coulda mouda.
It's a bum wearing three hats,
the high priest. He winks at us, falls asleep.

Let's not argue about drinking.
A young couple slide off their stools,
bump heads going out the door.

Ratburger, I say, chomping down
on one of the four I ordered.
Ratboogers, Kenny says.

Rats ain't got no boogers.
It's the plump woman behind the counter,
safe in her hair net.

Kenny punches the jukebox:
Mitch Ryder's "Little Latin Lupe Lu,"
and a couple old Motown.

Let's dance, Sugar, Kenny says.
The counter woman shakes her hips a little

but she clearly don't got the spirit:
What's that mean, Latin Loop De Lou?

It's a Christmas song, Kenny says.
The grill man with bad skin
laughs at that—his spit sizzles.

from *Time, Temperature*

1980. In the department store,
those foam packing chips that last forever
poured from an overhead funnel
into gift boxes full of vases, clocks, books,
ceramic dogs, martini glasses, china, silver.
To cushion and protect.

Kim's dark skin

surrounded by the white, white foam.
We worked in that blizzard together.
We leaned across the table toward each other
in the basement under the store
where all the black people worked,
along with me and another white kid.

We felt like robots down there,
filling and sealing. Till our eyes locked
in the hard stare of mannequins.
We ate lunch together
in the lounge. People talked.
It only took me a year to ask her out.
Dixie scowled. *What are you doing?*
This is Detroit you're talking about.

We went to a movie in my part of town,
for coffee in her part.
I can't remember what we saw
because I held her hand in the dark
and we were alone there just like
two white kids, or two black kids.

All night the stares bit into us
like tiny bugs we couldn't see.
Walking to the car, I squeezed
her hand into a fist.
I guess you have to be rich
to get away with it, she said
and maybe she was right.

Our own sizzling skins could not
our own good fire could not blend
or overwhelm or distract or soothe enough.

We were not rich enough or fast enough, fat enough
or thick-and-thin enough. We could not slam
our car doors loud enough to break the long stare.

In her apartment, her child cried
upstairs while we held each other on the couch.

Go home white boy, somebody yelled
when I got in my car.

At work the next day
the foam rained down between us.
It lay in heaps.
I couldn't look at her.
I grabbed two handfuls and squeezed:
nothing can destroy them.

St. Peter Claver

Every town with black Catholics has a St. Peter Claver's.
My first was nursery school.
Miss Maturin made us fold our towels in a regulation square
    and nap on army cots.
No mother questioned; no child sassed.
In blue pleated skirts, pants, and white shirts,
we stood in line to use the open toilets
and conserved light by walking in darkness.
Unsmiling, mostly light-skinned, we were the children of the
    middle class, preparing to take our parents' places in a
    world that would demand we fold our hands and wait.
They said it was good for us, the bowl of soup, its
    pasty whiteness;
I learned to swallow and distrust my senses.

On holy cards St. Peter's face is olive-toned, his hair
    near kinky;
I thought he was one of us who pass between the rich and poor,
    the light and dark.
Now I read he was "a Spanish Jesuit priest who labored for
    the salvation of the African Negroes and the abolition
    of the slave trade."
I was tricked again, robbed of my patron,
and left with a debt to another white man.

Blackbottom

When relatives came from out of town,
we would drive down to Blackbottom,
drive slowly down the congested main streets
    —Beaubien and Hastings—
trapped in the mesh of Saturday night.
Freshly escaped, black middle class,
we snickered, and were proud;
the louder the streets, the prouder.
We laughed at the bright clothes of a prostitute,
a man sitting on a curb with a bottle in his hand.
We smelled barbecue cooking in dented washtubs,
    and our mouths watered.
As much as we wanted it we couldn't take the chance.

Rhythm and blues came from the windows, the throaty voice of
    a woman lost in the bass, in the drums, in the dirty down
    and out, the grind.
"I love to see a funeral, then I know it ain't mine."
We rolled our windows down so that the waves rolled over us
    like blood.
We hoped to pass invisibly, knowing on Monday we would
    return safely to our jobs, the post office and classroom.
We wanted our sufferings to be offered up as tender meat,
and our triumphs to be belted out in raucous song.
We had lost our voice in the suburbs, in Conant Gardens,
    where each brick house delineated a fence of silence;
we had lost the right to sing in the street and damn creation.

We returned to wash our hands of them,
to smell them
whose very existence
tore us down to the human.

Mark Donovan

HIP 1

it's seven-thirty and soon
it will be time to go
to the poetry reading, so
I have to pick out a few
poems, but I don't want to
look through the old poems
because I know all those
and they don't say what
I want to say today
and I'll try to write a
new one, but the dude
behind me has been cutting
his lawn in the rain for
an hour, reminding me
that this suburban life
runs a little short of paradise
and compares closer to the
cass corridor than most
successful young families would
admit to, and you know
how strange it can be for me
to be here as it is to be there

●◆●

HIP 2

Here we find horizons in poetry
Here we find the continuation
of the tribal ritual of storytelling
song handed down and changed
only to meet the needs of civilization

Gloria Dyc

Cargo of Grace

Finally the ships return to the river
I had almost given up hope this long winter
they signal to me in their baritone
adding resonance to the most mundane acts
Only a month ago the icy banks lost their moorings
and I read of a dog rescued from a floe
by two men with compassion and a canoe in storage
Often I've imagined the shock of the cold water to the dog
how quickly he must have relinquished the image of a bird
as he struggled that evening for a footing
And I've imagined the curious light in the eyes of the dog
as he might have turned for a moment from his rescuers
to the terrible vacuum that would have been his
Now the congestion of the lakes has been conveyed down
a river the color of an eel
a river relentless and austere as a plant
Finally the ships return and signal to me
I reel to the banks as if stunned by fever
greedily I unload their cargo of grace

On Seeing Old Friends in Detroit

They've lit a bonfire
in the center of a vacant lot

another old mansion razed
the phone book half the size
it was twenty years ago when
idled workers sniped at Japanese cars
from the dark rim of I-94
I return from the West each year
to survey the remains of the city
stark in the still grey
of a post-industrial age
I sense the slow digestion
of cigarette paper, shards of glass
in the patient Michigan earth
And around the fire are old friends
faces leaner and broken in
like the old leather jackets they wear
They move in a magnetic field
of survival and familiarity
there is laughter and cryptic talk

And you, my friend:
under the bulk of your clothes
and your fuller beard
there appears to be new weight
but . . . you won't talk to me
In the kitchen of this Victorian
with those high ceilings and walls
perfect for large-scaled art
you evade, succumb to the gravity
of old bonds, comfortable and worn
as your field coat, your jeans
You look for another bottle
in the walk-in pantry
the host, now in AA, turns you on
to a bottle of stashed brandy

You open and swig
I ask: *You're a father now?*
It's strange, you respond, and turn away
feeling the pull of the Morse code
and friends with long-necked Stroh's
Some remark about the city is a trigger:
This is not post-industrial
or even post-modern
This city is a memory, you say
We are near the university:
twenty-five years ago
I'd walk these streets
weaving through professors and pimps
those tedious socialists hawking papers
I wore a long, yellow coat
over a very short, neon dress
I was majoring in theater
Do you remember how we talked
about French surrealism
how together we read André Breton
made love in your apartment
using a pillow on the floor
while your girlfriend was at work
her clothes, her smell so close?
God . . . I'd like to go back and live again
that sex we had in the dusty theater
of Old Main standing up against the wall
my skirt pushed up, and then caught
without my diaphragm, you pulled out
and I swear when you came
we could hear a spat on the floor
We were young; you shared a rhapsody
about your work on the mailboat
the Detroit river and its moods
the churches on the banks

and the stark beauty of factories
I would trace the pattern of hair on your chest, your navel

We circle the remains of cake and cheese
on the dining room table
at the end of the year's longest night
We burn brightly now, yet soften and retreat
like the candles that have burned
all night in the tall windows
Surely the earth will turn back
and we can expect day-by-day
some small gift of light
We cup this small hope like a flame
and slip away, snubbing ritual
After the gathering, I have a dream:
these are the end times
I am in line, waiting
almost out of time and money
there are few items on the shelves
I could be in a store in Poland
Then I am at a university
my students show up, wild-eyed
I try to go on as usual
though I sense the menace
they draw out bottles and knives
hidden in layers of clothing
I am defenseless
my skin is transparent
the casing over sausage
I am filled with dark rot
as I stumble down a dark staircase
of the last years of the 20th century
The earth has broken out of its orbit!
Alarmed, I dream I am dying
My friends: *we are all dying.*

Henrietta Epstein

Confession of the Rouge Park Killer

. . . Then the Lord said to Cain, "Why are you so angry and cast down?" Genesis

My father never taught me
how to hunt . . .
He liked to brag about
his luck in California
before his business failed
and I was born;
before Sault Ste. Marie,
the fuckin' War
which broke him, sent him down
here to Detroit
to choke in factories.

His weekend sport was quail.
By morning he'd be gone,
leaving me behind
chained to my mother.
By night I was her jailer,
fleshing her hunger
till he returned—with nothing!
to find her trained,
a huntress, crouched
in their half-empty bed.

He died hunting,
groping for air;
one shattered duck still tied
in his bleeding sack.

Wedding Photograph: Detroit 1935

There is not a flower anywhere.
The bride, my mother, sits cross-legged
on a rented silk upholstered bench
wearing a black dress, black silk stockings
and delicate buckled shoes.
Her raven black hair is bobbed around her blanched cheeks,
her onyx eyes look out at nothing in this world.
She is thinking of her mother, eight years dead
for whom she is dressed in mourning.
She is afraid that her bridegroom's hand,
which rests lightly on her shoulder,
will firm its grip on her flesh,
or even worse, slide down
and make its claim upon her breast.
She is afraid of the photographer, whose head
is hidden beneath a wide black sheet,
afraid of what he sees
through the mysterious glass eye that is focused
on her and the man standing behind her.

The bridegroom, my father, is smiling
at the photographer's bidding,
even though he is thinking of the rent unpaid
on their apartment in Chicago
and of the wedding ring, unpaid for
in the pocket of his new suit, unpaid for.
His palm on his bride's shoulder grows damp,
and later a small stain will appear
in the satin panel of her dress.
He wants her to know that he never meant
to let things pile up against him,
he wants her to know that he lied,
that although he threatened suicide,

he might not have drowned in Lake Michigan
had she refused him;
he wants her to know that the promises
he made to her brothers
were the core of his own dreams, not lies
as she had discovered them.

As their picture is snapped
and particles of unearthly light surround them,
the bride, my mother, will feel faint
and drive her fingernails into the silken seat
where later, the photographer will notice
the torn jagged shreds in the fabric.

Then the bride and groom will pass
through an archway to a room
full of brothers and sisters.
In the bride's dark eyes,
the assembled guests will alter,
will lose their wedding finery and become
the strangers gathered at the tracks
of the Hastings Avenue streetcar, where she,
returning home from school
had pushed through the crowd to find
her mother dead on a Friday afternoon,
the Sabbath candles fallen from her shopping bag.

Once the bride, my mother, and the groom, my father,
are seated at the long banquet table,
the rabbi and the guests will begin
the prayers over the wine and bread;
before they are finished, the bride
will rise from her place beside the groom,
she will slip from his grasp
and run to the center of the great hall,

her voice, high over their voices
will wail the prayer for the dead:
"Yis-gad-dal v'yis-kad-dash . . ."
her black-sleeved arms flailing before her.
"Oh, Mamma, Mamma, Mamma, why did you leave me alone?"

Linda Nemec Foster

Detroit

for Jan Zayti

A city like Detroit only exists in a prose poem. No stanza
or line break could contain it. But paragraphs—big blocks
of words—that's what Detroit is. Run-on sentences border
its streets, parking lots: heavy miles of guard rails and
fences. Cars live here: carburetors, catalytic converters,
automatic transmissions, power brakes, power steering, white
sidewalls, fuel injection, radiators, front suspension,
mufflers, bucket seats, leather, chrome, head room, leg room,
ride like a million, can we build one for you, the highways
of your mind, luxury ride, down 8 Mile, 7 Mile, 6 Mile,
5 Mile, down till they don't count no more, down to the
Renaissance Center, and the mass transit that nobody gives a
shit about, down to the very guts which is not blood or heart
or even steel but riding fast smooth down the leg of Woodward
Ave., windows open, radio blasting. Keeping alive.

Larry Gabriel

Cold Hands in the Urban Village

he wanted to leap
onto his bike
& drive her away
to a beautiful place
where there were trees
& they might walk about
& forget about time
on a beach
where the sunset
on those great
midwestern lakes
was enough to keep them
holding on to each other
as the sky darkened

he wanted somehow
to feel the earth's throb
between their hearts

Band of Gypsies

we danced endlessly
turning the record over
time after time

until each note was choreographed,
each move anticipated.

was the brothers listenin' to you?
shit man, that night you were god.

even later,
when just two of us
danced the mating ritual,
staccato machine gun blasts
rattled our hips.

the politicization
of melodic love

Crosstown Traffic

static chrome-glazed enigma
the past confronts you
like a nazi roadblock.
nothin' to do but
blast your way through.

the other side of town beckons:
something you'd give your life
to attain.

Egyptian Gallery in August: Detroit 1994

for those of us made homeless

Bring your body in, out of the heat.
You are safe, now, as long as you keep silent.
Like a dream, the museum remembers
    something you must know—
Hidden in stone, in air, in glass cases
    that reflect you back,
Making everything part of you.

Outside, pedestrians turn toward home.
They finger their keys like worry beads
    and try to remember which street is theirs
In the suffocating dusk.
    But you sense, if you wait long enough
The answer will come, not in words
    but in hieroglyphs cut so deep
You can read them even in the dark.

Yes, on an ancient pot, an aloe
    is bending in the breeze.
And above your head a god offers
    the dead the breath of life.
Move closer to a predynastic grave,
    the bones still curved in sleep, the objects
Waiting for their owner's touch again.

You kneel at the edge, you can almost
Smell jasmin. ASK IT!
"Do you remember me?"

Song in Tender Black

for Mrs. Nancy Price, Nursing Home Aide,
Highland Park, Michigan

Ladies named for flowers
Ladies pale as gauze
Looking for their mamas
Out of rooms with no doors.

Greying sons and daughters
Visit when they will—
Want to see them dignified,
Want to see them still.

Still beneath the bedsheets,
Still tied to a chair,
Still so all can see
Some aide has combed their hair.

But Price the onyx eagle
Waits upon her doves;
Moves like halls like music,
Gospel hymn of love.

She puts no stock in still life—
Her mama's ninety-two
Still singing in her garden
With plenty more to do.

JOAN GARTLAND   127

Now Price knows Jesus loves her,
All these daughters, too,
And resurrecting them
Is what the Lord would have her do.

She walks up close behind them
And whispers sweet as jazz,
"Come on Sugar, use the body
You have!"

Then inch by inch steel walkers
Advance across the floor;
Heads and canes are lifted up
Closed eyes meet light once more.

"Come on, Sugar, come on!"
The revolution starts.
Hear that "Come on, Sugar!"
Heal your heart.

On Leaving You

constant. cycle. once more.

Autumn ambrosia
fallen leaves. damp
compact. still-warm soil.

How was it toward the apocalypse
revelation. while i was with You

i felt.
as though i was that.

lonely D.O.T. bus driver.
who simply "does" the Red Loop?
brags about it. out of boredom.
being the only pilot on board.

Mindful of You
we should all be grateful.
to keep his spirits high.

The same. hour long voyage
downtown urban Sinbad. from
Dept. of Social Services. then
back again. 12X.

Dark skin cargo. locked in
lopsided Circle.
cannot swallow Itself.
for relief.

Walking. walking. into
the seams. of saturday night
of Michigan Ave

shadows. follow one another.

1 A.M. plus. loose change.

The solitary Moon shivers.
conceals her blue tear-stained
face. Storm sky Thunder rumble
the blues. hurl themselves.

shaking sense into the Earth.
as we once had conceived it.
before the birth
of that misguided
moment.

fall 1997

Dan Georgakas

Remembering Detroit 1973

nine turkeys ago
kennedy could not survive the bullets of the conspiracy
and my cancer-drained grandfather watched jack ruby
gun down lee harvey oswald
and thought it was the million-dollar movie
/that night he imagined the wagon master had come
for a final campfire coffee and that his own prodigal son
had finally learned to weep,
but as I watched his life ebb into the darkness
it was not like a movie at all
/this year i'm munching on bananas
instead of roasted drumsticks
and moving into a new apartment
without my wife of four years;
we carried our love
in to and out of a dozen such apartments
spread across two continents
only to have it pass into a darkness
as irrevocable as my grandfather's
/it ends without benefit
of cranberry sauce or chestnut stuffing;
it ends with clogged throats
and bravura masks
/and the conspiracies grow more desperate
and new kennedys can never be our champions

and our grandfathers are gone
and we no longer have the luxury
of blaming our failures
on broken Greek eggs
or a sour Puerto Rican palate
/i hear on the radio
that an international conglomerate
is sponsoring a new show called
the billion-dollar movie

October Song

They who never ruled before
poured from their factory districts
across the bridges of Petrograd
to make October.
The moon was so startled
all global tides
shifted.
The lights went on all over Europe.
Nothing
can ever be the same.

Charles A. Gervin

My Sister Chicken Recalls How She Listened to the Supremes on the Radio as a Young Girl

for Linda Joyce Gervin

Their voices seemed so large
That I studied them in regret
And wasted evenings after school
When the city seemed to sweat rain like tears
And I drug it in on home.

With the radio on, I applied
My makeup, and then washed it off,
Only to reapply it—so satisfied
With my new shell and skirt
While doing a few hip steps.

As I combed, then put the rollers
In my hair, all the lyrics—
Each subtle nuance of voice I knew by heart
From the very pace of the city
Until I could not tell their voices from my own.

Michele Gibbs

Message from the Meridian

You came to the right place.
It's just that ironweed and roses
bloom here now
the people having gone to seed.

Upturned earth
manured by passing cars
sprouts purple petals
growing in rhythm
to the devastation
of the wrecker's sweep.

Paradise Valley, this once was
where Black life hummed
flashing hues
flowers only dreamed of
swaying in the wind
of the sweetest horns outside heaven . . .

But that was then
when Black Bottom was a dance
and living
still held out a chance for change.

Ask anyone.

If you can find them
and they can speak.

Or failing that
pick a bouquet.
Carry it as a reminder
of lives lost, stolen, stray,
but maintaining their color
come what may.
Plant these flowers
and when someone asks,
"What are they?"
say,
"They only look like weeds.
In fact, they are the generation of tomorrow
growing in my garden
and they will not
be uprooted
again" . . .

Because back in this homegrown groove
being turned to rut
by powers what want it so,
we say no.
Who can't believe in it
should leave it alone.
We don't want
no historical markers designating graves
our ground
paved and replaced by parking lots
where no roses grow.

Even weeds gone to seed
breed trees

casting cool shade
to shelter weary souls.

The cracks
in sidewalks, walls, roofs, smokestacks,
have broken too many backs already
for we to be saying "yes"
to the latest attack
on our territory.
The helicopters
are now steady landing
on the miracle
of so many still standing.
But we,
veterans of domestic and foreign wars,
don't need no more walls
in our Valley
don't want our backyards
turned to alley
will not be roped in
by yet another Lt. Calley
proclaiming:
"We destroyed the village to save it."
Mother wit won't allow it
and we who live here
avow it for true:

This valley become the Bottom
Black and blue
will be Paradise again
no matter who,
with whatever "new"
thinks they have the right
to come through.

Someday

Someday
i'll write
my last Detroit poem —

when the echoes of Malcolm
at Greater King Solomon
no longer move in the air

when the last
full flattened fifth,
swallowed straight
down the last throat
open to the blue note of survival
rings no more

when Black Bottom
becomes Paradise again —
            maybe then.

when the last stricken mother
is done washing
the blood of her children
from the ground where they have fallen
with her tears
and a rainbow appears

when the real criminals are caught
and the beast of greed
born of spiritual need
be laid to rest
instead of the next of kin —
            maybe then.

when we finally get the news
'bout how our dues be used
and refuse
to be abused
anutha' futha'

when a good year
has nuthin' to do with tired rubber

when the hood
is a natural sanctuary again—
            maybe then.

when needles
are only used to sew clothes
and we emerge
robed in the whole cloth
of our future—
            maybe then.

but that day
is way off
around
a bend in a river
not clogged
with blood, bone,
Chief Pontchartrain's memory mixed with our own,
Tubman's tracks
showing us the way
South this time,
out of this stone cold clime.
Back beyond the way we came.

But as i say,

that day
is way off.

And until then,
while there is witness to bear,
work to share
and some people to care—
i'll be there.

Perri Giovannucci

Cadillac Dreams of the Detroit River

for Carlos E. Gonzalez Sardiña

The sun slips its yoke
behind Saskatchewan
and sends instead
the breath of reindeer;
their hooves pack the snow,
tighten its grip on the land—

sends instead the scent of pines.
See them on the far plain,
the size of matchsticks.
A crow is the only color
in the absence of all color.

At the old fort they
were cloaked as bears.
One dreamed that knives
bloomed at his sleeve ends.
The barrel of his musket
held the teeth in his head.

One dreamed of honeysuckle
that grew at the gate
of his mother's house.

You can clip the stem
and sip the essence like a straw.

He went for a drink
where the river slid like an eel
below the ice. He stood
on the surface like a saint.
The brush cleared his way
and his own limbs animated

the likeness of wildlife.
Voices filled the forest as if
it were the rafters of a church.
Men emptied their traps.
They took the skins but
they could not take the souls.

Maurice Greenia, Jr.

In 1996 & 1997 I drew over 500 drawings (in chalk) on all four sides (some one thousand feet) of the abandoned Hudson's building in downtown Detroit. This project was created in response to the fact that 60 artists were invited to paint murals on the building and soon enough all that work was destroyed/painted over: to the silence of the media & the art community. This poem is in memory of both my chalk-work and that of my fellow muralists and chalk collaborators. (A few other people were kind enough to contribute chalk-work to the Hudsons Project.)

Poem in Memory of Artworks on the Hudson's Building

load/by the power and pull of empty spaces
a huge spent cage encrusted with dust and sad echoes/ dead stars
    in the shadows
and billions of footsteps once chattered here/ nipped snaggles of silence
refugees invade and search for warm corners/ a shade of sheltered night
cobwebs/ the dirty plates of thieves and vultures smashed at the walls
the elevator shafts a dry infinity/ dead stairways form into tombstones
yet in the daybreak light pulls through the cracked glass/ sharply snarled
hundreds of rooms connect in confused friendship/ pulsing in unison
walls, floors and ceilings concoct hellos and goodbyes./ breaking the ice
trash, finality, refuse-refusals/ the stolen and the unwanted get in a hudo
a false step gets you there/ hurry and you'll twist your ankle into 1947
ghosts of cash registering, ringing/ the riff of finance's musical punctuat
a paper trail of paycheck's foodbills pecking at doorsteps/ taxable outcor

the sampling repetition of interlocking lives/ in day ins–day outs
this building echoes and sings with lodged emptiness/ and lost times
the future all used up/ the past like a phantom mist of days lost
the tip of a hat/ a handshake or a kiss or a kick or a salute or a gesture
and all that routine long lost/ ah the window displays of plastic plaster
      people in all their prominent finery and duds
eventually/ the artist was forced to confront all these then and now ghosts
pocketsful of shadows, echoes, goofs, heartbeats/ the painter's hand ignites
murals/ the display windows of the imagination of hand and paint
yapping at window of channel-shiftings/ detroit's stories thrown up on
      the wall in a spirit of gift-giving
then, this gift rejected/ erased and the erasure ignored
in the black-painted boards and windows/ an unstarred night sky called
a blackboard for lessons or experiments/ forming into a circle
in the round/ the square meets the hip in a circus of becoming images
the gonest party ended up erupting/ a circus of multicolor shades agiggled
impossible animals animate some silly paradise/ people who no one's ever
      seen try to talk them down or sing to them
these creatures join up with a building/ like entering a world
they cast their fate with the structure/ recklessly loyal to the bitter end
and children wonder about it all/ and various wander about it all
this temporary "free zone" where anything can happen/ and does
for magic's sake/ drawn in shadow and sunlight
the artist's hand/ ever changing colors as it guides and ignites the parade
the empty zone/ the audience is sparse and fragmented
yet the performance continues to build and complicate/ it comes alive
this secret world/ glows in the heart of downtown detroit
yet many never see it/ walk by without realizing what goes on these walls
hide in plain sight/ invisible in daylight in ways, at times
it grew/ up the ladder, the beanstalk, the blurry blue wings of chalk dust
and when it was full/ a cage grew around it
and a wall covered the cage/ and they bit and chewed at the building
and tried to suck some of the poisons out of it/ and gave it last rights
and put it under lock and key/ under guard and administration
and locked the artist out of his studio/ and tossed the residents onto

the streets, their home not their home
and denied the artist a chance to visit or acquire any of his work/ as
   the rain, wind, sun and workers erased it
and now the remnants prepare themselves to be exploded/ imploded
and kick contaminated dust/ all over the perimeter
yet when the building is lost/ and long gone
the strange artworks which once dwelled there/ will still live in photos
and in people's minds/ and the pink cow horse ridden by bird with
   tiny hat
will give way to huge-headed folk in business suits/ which will
give way to a conspiracy of impossible shapes/ which float like clouds
which will give way to a huge emptiness/ a huge hole perhaps to be
   refilled
with something or other/ which will give way to 9 foot tall people, laugh
which will give way to a hundred strange dancers frozen in space/ in mi
which gives way to a spark of air doing loop-de-loops/ playing amongst tl
   rubble and debris past the last blast of falling in
which gives way to the birth, death and rebirth mechanism/ over and ov
again and again/ as art talks to the city yet the city can't talk to art
as strange architectures dismantle soul's sole residue/ shadowed
   echoed songs.

Jim Gustafson

Jukebox

I would eat a jukebox if it made me fall in love
with my work again. These days I feel
like an obsolete Univac oddly replete
with a functional sciatic nerve and a massive erection
left out on the sunporch during the ice storm of the century.
There are memories and then there are mirrors.
Then there are mirrors shattered by concussion grenades,
concussion grenades that are launched
like rocket-propelled glockenspiels
through walls of salmon pate. They hit the expensive floors
and erupt with "Dancing in the Streets."
Don't forget the Motor City. No chance.
It's choral rapture, glossolalia for broke dick dogs,
weird howling by the guard shack,
a requiem for a complicated obsession
buried to its chin in succubi excreta.
I VOWED that I would eat a jukebox if it made me fall in love
with my work again. But I'm not going to rip out my heart,
trade it in for quarters, and entertain cheap strangers
no more no more no more no more. The vultures
are eating frozen quiche and the ospreys
are out of town on confidential business.
The law whores have turned everyone else into omnivores.
The passage of time has become an abhorrence to its ownself.
And listen, blubberbreath, I have a boot full

of ball bearings and a trunk full of dynamite,
and to be perfectly honest, I'm fresh out of mercy,
cheap or otherwise. The stupid tyrant
put me in charge of collecting the grog tax,
but I just collected the grog itself,
and now say spew on you, Stooge Rex.
I'm giving it all back to the peasants,
who have *earned* the right to stay drunk forever.
Yeah, yeah, vitriol is a terrific fat-buster.
And raw remorse will release the shredded angels
who have clogged your arteries.
And you too
will figure out
the joy
of variation
assuming you
live long enough
to get real.

Aurora Harris

Jitterbug, Jazz and the Graystone

In memory of James "Jitterbug" Jenkins and
the Graystone Ballroom

Blessed sound—
Is that why we're here James,
Jazz junkies, poets and patron saints
gathered to mentally genuflect in
the rhythms of your dream?
Is that why you wanted to keep it,
that Graystone scene, like G-Ma's recipe
for survival in bad times; love strained from The
Depression's pot of dandelion greens?
What made you want to keep them,
John Coltrane's piano, J. C. Heard's drums,
original music for Joe Williams by
Ernie Wilkins and those chairs,
instruments from the Gabriels and
those photos over there?
What placenta of night fed you?
Made you the spirit of a jazz-loving bird
that spread its wings for the rest of us to fly on?
Was it a black and white photo of
The Lady's head just so, neck strained, mouth open—
Billie caught in a moment of a mad blues pain
that reminded of bricks, riot heat in fading light,

that child you saw running from an angry mob of whites?
Was it the stop and start epistrophy of your
Dexter bus grind? The way they held their nickles
so they wouldn't have to touch you?
Blessed sound—
Wrapping you up in geodynamic forces
of what was under asphalt—
street car bones, Paradise Valley, the souls
of black folk echoing off the walls
of a Black Bottom hole
called "freeway to Downtown"
some societal displacement
that reaped travel from a field
that bulldozed right through them—
thick waterfall walls of swing and summer heat
smelling like grease and Joe Muer's garbage;
walleye, red snapper, pickeral spines and tails
cornmeal lard fried or made into soup,
clarinets and crooners, saxophones and bands
that set up their sets for a night at Henry's Swing Club,
Larks and The Three Sixes, excitement winding down at
Brown's or Freddy Guinyard's.
Is that what made you do it?
Or was it the songs of little black boys
with homemade wooden boxes
syncopating calls of " 'Scuse me, shoe shine, Mistuh?"

Blessed sound—
All that jazz in your head—
The Synco Jazz Band, I mean,
McKinney's Cotton Pickers: William with
Todd Rhodes, Milton Senior, Dave Wilbourn,
Claude Jones, Wesley Stewart and June Cole . . .
Fletcher Henderson with Coleman Hawkins, Rex Stewart,

Joe Smith and Buster Bailey . . . Jean Goldkette and
The Orange Blossoms: Don Redman, Prince Robinson,
James Dudley, Joyce Thomas, Langston Curl, Joe Smith,
John Nesbitt, Cuffee Davidson, Bob Escudero
and Todd Rhodes with Cuba Austin
tap dancing for the crowd.
Blessed sound, James Jitterbug Jenkins—
All those shoes in your head
dancing to society bands, hot big bands—
the swish of ball gowns and furs with mules
walking 'cross the floor, feet sliding and spinning,
tapping and kicking, jumping, jitterbugging, sound
bouncing off Graystone's Corinthian and mirrors,
shoes bouncing on a floor that sprung back from its springs
when Ellington and Lunceford had Battle of The Bands
after Goldkette opened doors for
black folks on Blue Mondays
'til dance, trying to live, hard work and car factories
sweat naps into conked heads.
Blessed sound—
That music on the radio, saving folks
like Jesus on migrations to the North.
Blessed sound James—
The silky jazz voices of Sarah Vaughn, Ella Fitzgerald
and Carmen McCrae.
All that love James—
Jitterbug Jenkins, are you listening to me?
Jazz junkies, poets and patron saints
are gathered to genuflect
in the rhythms of your dream.
James the jazz lover,
James the bus driver,
The man who dared
to love jazz that much,
who loved the memories of a dance hall enough

to want to save it.
Can you hear me Jitterbug?
James, are you listening?

Bill Harris

Get Off the Bus

"You know where Canfield at?"
"When you see me get off 2 more stops is your stop."
"I'm looking for Canfield and Cass."
"Parole office."
"I didn't do it."
"I been in jail plenty times. Sometimes I didn't do it. What didn't
    you do?"
"Possession of stolen property. It was my truck."
"Your truck?"
"It had been in the po-lice pound. And I had it."
"What was you doing with it?"
"It was mine."
"But it had been in the pound."
"Friend of mine left it by the house. I didn't ask him how he got it."
"Possession's 9/10s of the law. You had it when they found it."
"So?"
"So you go 2 more after you see me get off. Ask anybody from there."

Detroit Blues

big legged hefty hipped juicy bosomed kinda
bad ass
ass shakin
shakin em on down

down to the nitty gritty
gritty kinda
big legged hefty hipped juicy bosomed kinda
bad ass
ass shakin
shakin em on down
down to the nitty gritty
gritty kinda
De-troit blues.

Elegy

for Robert Hayden 1913–1980

Black bottom baby:
    Beaubien & Beacon blossom.
    As bewildered boy
witnessed the wicked,
the wondrous
    with weakened eyes.

In retrospect, where
    others only saw landscapes
    of blight and blues,
he reexamined
through lyric,
    metaphorical lens,

and painted
    kaleidoscopic praise songs
    of flowers
that bloomed in the night garden
of the valley
    called Paradise.

Kaleema Hasan

Envisioning Greed as Hope

Detroit as the intimate secret of my love,
a river of communities
flows down woodward avenue and
along west vernor highway   of course you see the people who live
    on the
            banks of gratiot and the grand river
        the flowing of female dresses, long, colorful, covering, short
and revealing
skin of ardent black   exquisite brown   ellingtonian red, whispers
    of white
and the men, their tails of prosperity mining the poverty from the
    meager monthly check
        the re-burial of less than pristine shoreline
        land scraped with what is less than pristine posterity,
        their tucks, tails, and long tradition of running from
        the love of women, or the love of children or the love of
        justice

Detroit, mack avenue is alive with your desperation
I understand that the current citizens have been employed to
carry their wealth from their stomachs to a bejewelled illusion upon
    your riverfront
a grand riverfront left silent by the left over greed of mercurial and
    leaded dumping,
a shoreline once lush with the dreams of native women the large
    footprints of an escaping army

of black slaves womens under the command of freed herself woman
   a shoreline nostalgic for the
incredible courage of men who stood as commanders of their labor,
   laying down their lives, lush
with the freedom that beats in the breast of humanity,

a grand riverfront reclaimed for the wealth that crystalizes poverty
   into a majestic idol of
forgotten charity, You have forgotten the blessings that silences the
   cries of the
children with warm houses, pure food, and neighborhoods of safety
   and love

You have forgotten
the profit that brings freedom
the very antithesis of greed

Robert Hayden

Elegies for Paradise Valley

I

My shared bedroom's window
opened on alley stench.
A junkie died in maggots there.
I saw his body shoved into a van.
I saw the hatred for our kind
glistening like tears
in the policemen's eyes.

II

No place for Pestalozzi's
fiorelli. No time of starched
and ironed innocence. God-fearing
elders, even Godless grifters, tried
as best they cold to shelter
us. Rats fighting in their walls.

III

Waxwork Uncle Henry
(murdered Uncle Crip)
lay among floral pieces

in the front room where
the Christmas tree had stood.

Mister Hong of the
Chinese Lantern (there
Auntie as waitress queened it
nights) brought freesias, wept
beside the coffin.

Beautiful, our neighbors
murmured; he would be proud.
Is it mahogany?
Mahogany—I'd heard
the victrola voice of

dead Bert Williams
talk-sing that word as macabre
music played chilling
me. Uncle Crip
had laughed and laughed.

IV

Whom now do you guide, madam Artelia?
Who nowadays can summon you to speak
from the spirit place your ghostly home
of the oh-riental wonders there—
of the fate, luck, surprises, gifts

awaiting us out here? Oh, Madam,
part Seminole and confidante
("Born with a veil over my face")
of all our dead, how clearly you
materialize before the eye

of memory—your AfroIndian features,
Gypsy dress, your silver crucifix
and many-colored beads. I see
again your waiting room, with its wax
bouquets, its plaster Jesus of the Sacred Heart.

I watch blue smoke of incense curl
from a Buddha's lap as I wait with Ma
and Auntie among your nervous clients.
You greet us, smiling, lay your hand
in blessing on my head, then lead

the others into a candlelit room
I may not enter. She went into a trance,
Auntie said afterward, and spirits
talked, changing her voice to suit
their own. And Crip came.

Happy yes I am happy here,
he told us; dying's not death. Do not grieve.
Remembering, Auntie began to cry
and poured herself a glass of gin.
Didn't sound a bit like Crip, Ma snapped.

V

And Belle the classy dresser, where is she,
who changed her frocks three times a day?
    Where's Nora, with her laugh, her comic flair,
      stagestruck Nora waiting for her chance?
Where's fast Iola, who so loved to dance
she left her sickbed one last time to whirl
in silver at The Palace till she fell?
    Where's mad Miss Alice, who ate from garbage cans?

Where's snuff-dipping Lucy, who played us 'chunes'
on her guitar? Where's Hattie? Where's Melissabelle?
Let vanished rooms, let dead streets tell.

Where's Jim, Watusi prince and Good Old Boy,
who with a joke went off to fight in France?
Where's Tump the defeated artist, for meals or booze
daubing with quarrelsome reds, disconsolate blues?
Where's Les the huntsman? Tough Kid Chocolate, where
is he? Where's dapper Jess? Where's Stomp the shell-
shocked, clowning for us in parodies of war?
Where's taunted Christopher, sad queen of night?
And Ray, who cursing crossed the color line?
Where's gentle Brother Davis? Where's dope-fiend Mel?
Let vanished rooms, let dead streets tell.

VI

Of death. Of loving too:
Oh sweet sweet jellyroll:
so the sinful hymned it while
the churchfolk loured.

I scrounged for crumbs:
I yearned to touch the choirlady's hair,
I wanted Uncle Crip

to kiss me, but he danced
with me instead;
we Balled-the-Jack
to Jellyroll

Morton's brimstone
piano on the phonograph,

laughing, shaking the gasolier
a later stillness dimmed.

VII

Our parents warned us: Gypsies
kidnap you. and we must never play
with Gypsy children: Gypsies
all got lice in their hair.

Their queen was dark as Cleopatra
in the Negro History Book. Their king's
sinister arrogance flashed fire
like the diamonds on his dirty hands.

Quite suddenly he was dead,
his tribe clamoring in grief.
They take on bad as Colored Folks,
Uncle Crip allowed. Die like us too.

Zingaros: Tzigeune: Gitanos: Gypsies:
pornographers of gaudy otherness:
aliens among the alien: thieves,
carriers of sickness: like us like us.

VIII

Of death, of loving,
of sin and hellfire too.
Unsaved, old Christians
gossiped; pitched

from the gambling table—

Lord have mercy on
his wicked soul—
face foremost into hell.

We'd dance there, Uncle
Crip and I,
for though I spoke
my pieces well in Sunday School,

I knew myself (precocious
in the ways of guilt
and secret pain)
the devil's own rag baby doll.

Errol A. Henderson

Support Your Local Police:
What We Pay Our Police For?

Malice was Greeeeeeeeen
and he didn't know.
—spent too much time on that pipe
his fingers couldn't even come apart; like they was pried closed
police couldn't see the dope
but they'd seen him with that white woman awhile before.

i mean, but how he have the nerve to have his fingers so tight
and what the hell was he doing with tight fingers that late at night
and all that stuff about a flashlight
shit, he lucky they didn't shoot him on sight
what we pay our police for?

now that Jose cat on the southwestside
talking trash to hook in the bar outside
they screamed at him to put his hands up high
now they in Southwest Detroit
how should they know he a Hispanic guy?
and they was black police so you know it wasn't no racial brutality
or nothin like that
but Jose had no business not doing what he was told
and that's just the fact

i mean, what was he doing out that late at night
and what was he doing not knowing how to speak English right

he was lucky they only shot him five times
i mean, what we pay our police for?

a 16 year old running through a vacant lot
Gary Glenn knew he was spose to be
in the Youth Home the day he was shot
now he hadn't caught a serious case
it was just that he was a habitual type runaway
and thank god that the police have guns!
and if he didn't do nothing then why did he run?
police had to shoot him six times
cause they thought he was strapped
as his mama screamed "don't shoot my boy no more"
what could they do but keep busting caps in his back

but what was Gary Glenn doing out in the daylight?
the daylight sun can blind just like it was midnight
and though he was shot in the back and no gun was found
by running away he could've still taken them innocent policemen
        down
i mean, what we pay our police for?

i was 9 years old in my brewster project bed
71 was hot before Boyd and Bethune was shot dead
and we was under the Big 4 and under STRESS
hook shot first or put you under cardiac arrest

and a gun was put to my mother's head
and a gun was put to my brother's head
a carbine was placed in my face
as i sat up in my bed
reading a Richie Rich comic book
i stared and waited to be dead

but what was I doing in my bed that night?

you know criminals often choose under bedspreads to hide
and who knows what kind of stories
my mother might've been reading me at bedtime
and what the hell we pay our police for?

Barbara Henning

As a Corrective

An urban story with a lonely man, two deceiving women and the
   promise of money.
Unfortunately, he left one day too soon, one hour too late.

As the owner of the Second Avenue Deli approached the bank
   machine, they shot him.
On a very windy day in Tompkins Square, the trees waving, the cab
   driver at the light,

a large blonde-haired woman in a black jacket, carries a shopping
   bag,
and two men with tammies on their heads and envelopes under their
   arms

shuffle along. Slipping out of the house to buy a bottle of cough
   syrup with a
forged prescription she was fined $30,000 for 954 unpaid parking
   tickets.

He got a ticket for driving thirty over the speed limit.
My mother kept me on a leash in the backyard.

The doctor told me to bring the unconscious man to her office
in a taxi. His worst crime was that he was homosexual.

A headache lands like a bird with sharp claws. Behind an empty lot, on the back of a building, DETROIT, in capital letters.

Garcia's Market

on Michigan by Trumbull

saturday morning

time for provisions
and old island men
to talk
  ay señor, que hay de nuevo
  o como está . . .
  todo es viejo . . . nada es nuevo

they begin the chat so

while deft fingers of island woman
search dasheen, tanya
casaba, maybe
ah . . . christopheen

but
little nose of
la morena
finds the prize

smell of salt and sea

bacalao

she knows real dreams will come
from bacalao
if moistened by aceite

a special combination
for la morena
to see sun
on dark saturdays

and all times when the sea is far

Quiet Battles

"All these things
make a woman,"
he said
while beating my stirrings
and bruising my hopes.

I listened for a long time,
but raged my rage
through inner ears that echoed

    I dream
    I dream

I acted for a long time
but raged my rage
through sinews that flexed and tensed
    I dreamt
    I dreamt

I smiled for a long time
but raged my rage
through teeth that whispered

    I'll dream
    I'll dream

These quiet battles added
full to my soul.

So I prettied my heart
and smartened my face
. . . and I survived.

I survived.

Jerry Herron

The Passion of Edsel Ford

1893–1943
a fiction

i

I was Edsel Ford when I was alive,
Henry Ford's only—acknowledged—child:
That day in the car, with the reporter, and Mr. Bennett,
(God, what a mess the War was, poor Mr. Roosevelt, so frail)
Father, of course, too, Mr. Bennett driving, and the man asked, the
        reporter I mean,
Who it was Father admired the most of all the men he'd ever met,
        and he said,
        That man right there.
And the reporter looked at me expecting me to—what?
Beam pleasure, I suppose. But I knew better.
Him, I mean, Father said (he enjoyed this), hooking his thumb in
        Mr. Bennett's
        direction.
At the wheel. That man right there.
(That little man, head of the Service Department—Father named
        it—with his
        thug operatives, and his secrets, and his guns, the only man I
        hated, truly
        hated. Father knew. I think Harry Bennett wanted to kill Mr.
        Reuther at

the overpass that day. There were others too. Other men had
    died.)
It was an awkward moment, then, the poor man, the reporter, not
    knowing
    what to do
    With his eyes.
But I knew. I'd done it before.
Lots of times.

ii

I was Edsel Ford when I was alive,
And I could look up at the Guardian, that building I had made.
    Cathedral of
    Finance, I kept the clipping in my wallet, the *News* called it that,
    thirty
    -six stories, *ebullient,* they said that too.
Father had no hand in it. I loved to see the flag—on top—reveal
    itself to the
    air, dream that solitude.
Open then, Oh! glorious year 1929—until.
Father called us to meet on Sunday morning—the board room (he
    was
    particular), top floor, rubbed his finger over the marble, sniffed
    at the
    air, odd, he'd never been there before—me, Kanzler,
The rest. All the partners. We knew what the President Mr. Hoover's
    man had
    asked Father to do,
To say he'd back the Guardian deposits, stand by the rest of the banks
    too, in
    Detroit. That was all, just *say* he would.
So people would know.

Like they'd done in Chicago. It stopped the run.
Father said he was buying his boy out of his troubles, that's what he
    called me,
    his boy, but as for the rest, they could go to jail, or to the devil,
    for all he
    cared.
Looked them in the eye and said it.
Not that we'd, any of us, done anything the rest weren't doing too.
    (Kanzler
    assured me, my brother-in-law.)
Let the crash come, Father said. And it did. The Guardian failed, all
    the other
    banks with it. They blamed us. Some said otherwise, but I knew.
The people blamed us. I saw it in their eyes.

iii

I was Edsel Ford, and Diego Rivera knew who I was. When I was
    alive.
Dr. Valentiner asked him here, to paint murals for the courtyard at
    the Art
    Institute.
But he hadn't the money to pay.

So I paid. It was 1932.
Señor Capitalist, Rivera called me, and inquired as to my knowledge
    of Marx.
    Did I know his friend Trotsky?
I didn't like him then, though Dr. Valentiner assured us he was a
    genius.
I paint you some pictures to show people who you really are, Señor
    Capitalist.
That's what he told me, standing on his scaffold.

His belly rode up when he laughed, beneath his belt, like something
    was
    pushing it from below.
They wouldn't let the people see, but I saw. Because I was paying.
Behind the drapes, with klieg lights.
(Do painters work at night? He did.)
So, today you'll show me *your* work, Señor Capitalist, he said one
    day.
And I told him to get in and we drove to the studio,
And I rolled out the big drawings, on the blackboard, of the new
    Lincoln, and
    I showed him.
And he looked a long time and then said he was ready to go.
I see you now, Señor Capitalist, so I know what to paint. I paint your
    father
    too.
I liked him then.
He finished his work at the Art Institute and left town, in the Spring,
    with
    Frida.
(I never liked her at all.)
They said it was time to take down the drapes, but I said No.
Not yet.
I wanted to know what he had seen. I wanted to see too. By myself.
I looked at Father, in the painting, on the walls, and at me, and I saw
    finally.
The people came.
They hated the murals, called them dirty, spiteful. Said they were
    ugly.
Paint over them, people said.
I didn't care.
Because I knew he'd seen. Rivera, I mean.

iv

I was Edsel Ford and I was alive. All that time ago.
In old J. L. Hudson's house, he was dead by then, had been dead for
    years.
Waiting for my love, dearest love, she was just eighteen, in her Uncle
    Hudson's
    parlor.
All that darkness there, the weight, the ugly chairs.
And Ellie finally coming down the stairs. (How could she have
    grown up here?)
She called my name, the name she called me, never Edsel, the
    name that
    Father gave me, after his school friend.
She called me Ned.
It's cruel to me now. To remember.
I'd have so long to miss her, and the boys, and Josephine.
My oldest, Henry II, only 25, in the Navy now, in the War.
There'll be no pain, they told her, the doctors, I could hear, but
    couldn't
    speak. The morphine saw to that.
But I knew, what they thought I didn't, about the cancer, thought
    they'd spare
    me, because I was weak, feared I'd cry, because I did cry
    sometimes.
He's dying, you see. And the fever just makes it worse, that he got
    from the
    milk his father sends from Fair Lane.
Father loved the taste, wouldn't let them sterilize it or use the
    pasteurizer.
    Make the boy drink it, he told them. It'll set him right.
So I slept, or they thought I slept. I could see the lake, St. Clair, from
    my bed, in
    our room, I could smell the spring. Last spring. Oh, Ellie.
And then one morning, when I was alone, it was over.

And then I wasn't Edsel Ford any more. I wonder that I had ever
   been.
Now I would have eternity not to be.

v

I was Edsel Ford when I was alive, the most alive, on the river, in the
   morning.
(He'll be there soon, just left, he's taken the launch this morning:
   Rouge River
      Plant, world's largest industrial facility. Newspapers said
   that, never me.)
         But not yet.
I liked being alive then, on the water by myself. Alone.
Because I could always see it in their eyes. Mr. Edsel, they'd say.
   Everyone
      being kind.
But I knew. How could I not know?
Know what, though?
That we were all just playing? That as soon as I was gone, and
   nobody would
      have to play at having Mr. Edsel around, they could all go back
   to being
      real. Just themselves.
And what would I be? I'd still have to play at being Edsel Ford.
Because I didn't remember what it was like when I wasn't there.
That's why I love the water, on the way down river, in the morning,
   to the
Rouge.
I was not Mr. Edsel then.
I was just
Free.

The Heidelberg Project

We're walkin' down to Jaybo's, see.
Just walkin'.
And we turn down by where
that boy got his nose sliced off
and they put it up his you-know-what?
That street there?

Well some guy gone and dump
about ten dozen of old shoes
right there on the street.
Right *on* the street.

It was on TV.
Not just the news.
It's been on "Oprah."

The guy, he says it's art.
Them old shoes.
Dump on the street.
Don't give me that shit.

They closed all the art.
Shut it down to save money.
If it was art, sister,
it would be locked up inside,
where couldn't nobody see it.

Edward Hirsch

Three Journeys

Whoever has followed the bag lady
on her terrible journey past Food Lane's Supermarket,
and Maze's Records, and The Little Flowering Barbershop
on the southeast corner of Woodward and Euclid
will know what it meant for John Clare
to walk eighty miles across pocked and jutted
roads to Northborough, hungry, shy of strangers,
"foot foundered and broken down" after escaping
from the High Beech Asylum near Epping Forest.
And whoever has followed the bag lady
on her studious round of littered stairwells
and dead-end alleys, and watched her combing
the blue-and-white city garbage cans for empties,
and admired the way that she can always pick out
the single plate earring and one Canadian dime
from a million splinters of glass in a phone booth
will know how John Clare must have looked
as he tried to follow the route that a gypsy
had pointed out for him, scaling the high
palings that stood in his way, bruising
his feet on the small stones, stooping to
admire the pileworts and cowslips, scorning
the self-centered cuckoos but knowing the sweet
kinship of a land rail hiding in the hedgerows.

I began this morning by standing

in front of the New World Church's ruined storefront;
I was listening to the bag lady and a pimply-
faced old drunk trading secrets with the vent man,
and remembering how a gentleman on horseback
had mistaken John Clare for a broken-down haymaker
and tossed him a penny for a half-pint of beer.
I remembered how grateful he was to stand
elbow to elbow in the Old Plough Public House
happily sheltered from a sudden rainfall.

But later when I saw the bag lady
sprawled out on a steaming vent for warmth
I remembered how Clare had moved on, crippled
by tiny bits of gravel lodged in his shoes,
and how he tried to escape from the harsh wind
by lying down in an open dike bottom
but was soaked through clear to his bones;
how he came to the heavy wooden doors
of the Wild Ram Public House hours later,
and gazed longingly at the brightly lit windows,
and had no money, and passed on. Whoever
has stood alone in the night's deep shadows
listening to laughter coming from a well-lit house
will know that John Clare's loneliness was unbending.
And whoever has felt that same unbending loneliness
will also know what an old woman felt today
as she followed an obedient path between the huge
green garbage cans behind Kroger's Supermarket
and the small silver ones behind Clarence's grocery.

I began this day by following a bag lady
in honor of John Clare but suddenly, tonight,
I was reading "The Journey Out of Essex, 1841,"
in honor of the unknown bag lady.
I had witnessed a single day in her life

and was trying hard not to judge myself
and judging myself anyway.
I remember how she stooped to rub her foot;
how she smiled a small toothful grin
when she discovered a half-eaten apple;
how she talked on endlessly to herself
and fell asleep leaning against a broken wall
in an abandoned wooden shed on Second Avenue.
Tonight when I lie down in the dark
in my own bed, I want to remember
that John Clare was so desperately hungry
after three days and nights without food
that he finally knelt down, as if in prayer,
and ate the soft grass of the earth,
and thought it tasted like fresh bread,
and judged no one, not even himself,
and slept peacefully again, like a child.

Ann Holdreith

Birth

Cold steel piston's grease
halo of shrine captured by
industrial saints
grind us through your rusty lathe.
Artists born from persistent gray.

To Mary

I've saved your doodles, those neat, small, undersea
creatures whose big eyes propelled them along the sea bottom

their direction unknown, their goal uncertain,
just creatures worried about splashes from above.

Me too, love. Those are mountains falling and beasts
we're still to meet are leaping in the sea.

Falling

Walking on basketballs to Woodward,
the soft uncertain feet, "Touch,
come down, settle, anchor your ankles,
for God's sake, the ground will hold you!"

but it will not rise or open,
nor any hand or hook or clutch
of circumstance beyond belief
make a next step the likely one.

And you will run, and you will fall,
not as you think, the Fall Voluptuous,

drifting like pollen down,
nor the Fall Pensive, pondered well,

but the Fall Stunning, running for the bus—
O tumble like a pin pulled free!—
and again you're glad to be flat,
as the air is let out of everything.

Ugolino of Detroit

Hear the *whang-whang* of the door closed in,
the burly, weary workman who nails my life down
and shuts the light forever on me?

Well, I have supplies and no children,
and I won't miss the Great Tire or Filthy Park,
but I wish I had a certain head to chew on

and a visitor to tell my story to
in tercets that would wound him like a pin,
because I'm not nice now, nor have I ever been.

Born on Slow Knives

1

born on slow knives
discreetly purchased
flowers love to feel us
becoming themselves
in the jaws of
the redoubtable maggot

2

abandoned car night
dead in the trunk
your business
and none of it
all of the windows
smashed and blind
as plastic now
just the light comes
through no shadows

3

beeping pumping
above sterile floors and viruses

mutated for sterility
the plug is in
the liquids monitored
data flowing
which end of the bargain
can you hold
in the dark red
glow of headless machines

4

the factory is going to roll
a parking lot over your house
the owners know they can count
on public servitude

the mayor's bank account
is coded with shit
green presidential
stains that read
fuck you and then some
amen and again

whenever the body
of the undead desires

there is an x
on your door

5

the sky is filthy with air
because some things
burn like dirt

there was a meeting
for explanation
of the body
only the hole for
breathing was missing

the reporters read their
sandwiches and ate
the PR packets
so there is no news
unless you sift toilet water
or believe them

6

you're going to die anyway
they said it on television
it is not the fault of your receiver
listen and repeat
if this had been an actual
emergency
the doors trapped
in your soul
the doors crusted over
with sugar and radiation
would have swung open
into your lungs
a corridor
and then an abyss
not just the nightmare
but the dream come true
losing the earth
losing the great blue curve
smelling smoke

Clark Iverson

Where I Grew Up

Walking toward the river
Under clear sky
We saw peeking
Between houses
Seven smokestacks
And two beside,
Still looming
In my secret places
And yours.

Dudley Randall

Pushed through a crack in earth
your eyes burn fire, soft as soft
your vision of cities: Green Apples, Roses
and Revolution.

You find the green moss discover north
tie square knots to hold our world together
press the pressure points to keep us
from bleeding on city streets.

In Paradise Valley, your man
Caruso flashes the ruby stick-pin,
stands on his chair
talks about being colored.

Prophet Jones sashays
to his temple on Hague.
Floats to the pulpit in her ermine robe,
Hands outstretched for alms.

Casablanca shadows Orchestra Place,
touts his basement palace, a place to look at cards,
have a taste or two.

You catch the mellow harmony
of their beat

siphon time, bottle it, then
uncork and stick it in our eye.

8 *Ball in Side Pocket*

Soft Side of Hastings, Oakland Avenue,
Wilfred's Billiard Parlor jammed between
The Pig Bar-B-Q and the Echo Theatre.

Slick Herman chalks his cue with resolution,
blue powder whispers to the floor.
He misses an easy bank shot in the corner.

Safe Eddie would always leave you on the rail
or hidin' behind balls you didn't want to shoot.
And steady Jerome looks for nonbelievers.
Hasn't missed a bank shot in four days.

Silent Ambrose shoots 9 ball
with Ralph, the Merchant.
Ralph accuses Silent of moving his balls
for a better angle, calls Silent a name.

Silent flashes quicker-than-light
2 inches of switchblade to Merchant's jugular.
In the stop-stillness of the moment,
you could hear a rat piss on cotton,
Don't you ever call me that . . . ever.

Silent wins the 9 ball game by forfeit.
Merchant can't find a cue
that will sit still in his hand.

Giant

that day Johnson shot the man in cold blood
his bible & small frame house
just blending in with the crowd—
& when he saw his cousin cut in pieces
& strewn down a Mississippi road
he was five & vulnerable to several obstacles

out in leafy Auburn Hills
a guy got $46 million from the deal
—figuring by this proxy statement—
& expect no trouble: Mercedes won't stand con-
    tamination

most just want to keep coming every day
& his fast-talking lawyer said: *Walter P.*
& damnit we're still too close to see the thing
all this rot jamming the frequencies
15,000 hurt & "an unknown number dead"
sympathy grew when word got around

—just took things in his own hands—
a man & woman down already
it was just the fifteenth of July
& the tropical tomb's noise was deafening

I wonder if members got to vote
hear the whole deal's worth $36 billion
"the marriage partners differ starkly in culture"
& a whole generation of stupid ideas
lay shredding at the gilded altar

small producers must form their own alliances
"known for decades as ponderous,
slow-moving, intensely conservative"
—& as competition escalates
the marriage promises immediate access
without diluting the carefully cultivated upscale image—

we've got to burn off the modern grinder's rough edges
every shift the filters get clogged
& Ashlock picks up a pinion gear
& says he's going to smash Scott's brains out
& they went for an injunction & got it

—& the judge gave him $75 a week
retroactive to the day of the shooting—

The Blab of the Pave

this is something besides a portrait
walls hum & drip on silver
metal quiet drapes dark floors

—he reads Adam Smith & is happy
to work 60 hours a week—

romantic fixations fall by the wayside
as her perfect sentences wax nostalgic

the visage rolls by like a train
balls of hay bouncing down the street
—you should have seen it—
the windows all lit & red toys on display

✻

we talk about music
but not about t.v.
a cogent idea a bell instead of a buzzer

today K's mother-in-law
a cloth merchant from Dakar
stares across a plate of chickens wishing in
      Wolof

✻

—well he'd better hurry
tell him he can take the freeway down—
with this weather he'd better be careful
—look just now for instance—
a pair of white eyes suddenly crowds out
      dreams
while you're splashing around
in front of that damned hospital
or along the school wall
ribs? who said ribs! one will be fine
you can't go east these days: it's blocked

✻

all afternoon the mushy yellow rice
was the backdrop for our wandering
while yearning lurked beside the diverted glances

& everybody got suddenly busy
there go the bells & buzzers again
the cup's crumbs swirl endlessly
hours pass by & nobody notices

Stephen Jones

A Rose for Brian

In memory of b.p. Flanigan—poet, botanist, journalist and raconteur

Same old shit, different day,
Or so, at least, it seems.
Another grief to weigh
On scales that balance dreams
Against the jagged truth
Of life. Another friend to bid
Farewell. How will we soothe
This wretched wound? You hid
Your love sometimes behind
Hard-ass jive; but we weren't fooled,
And we weren't blind
To your brawling tenderness, schooled
In raw realities of the street
And gentle wisdom of the heart.
You leave us incomplete,
But better. Not a bad start.
    You keep your head down brother.
    Who loves your ugly ass, motherfucker?

Lawrence Joseph

Curriculum Vitae

I might have been born in Beirut,
not Detroit, with my right name.
Grandpa taught me to love to eat.
I am not Orthodox, or Sunni,
Shiite, or Druse. Baptized
in the one true Church, I too
was weaned on Saint Augustine.
Eisenhower never dreamed I wore
corrective shoes. Ford Motor Co.
never cared I'd never forgive
Highland Park, River Rouge, Hamtramck.
I memorized the Baltimore Catechism.
I collected holy cards, prayed
to a litany of saints to intercede
on behalf of my father who slept
through the sermon at 7 o'clock Mass.
He worked two jobs, believed
himself a failure. My brother
believed himself, my sister denied.
In the fifth grade Sister Victorine,
astonished, listened to me recite
from the Book of Jeremiah.
My voice changed. I wanted women.
The Jesuit whose yellow fingers
cracked with the stink of Camels

promised me eternal punishment.
How strange I was, with impure thoughts,
brown skin, obsessions.
You could tell by the way I walked
I possessed a lot of soul,
you could tell by the way I talked
I didn't know when to stop.
After I witnessed stabbings
outside the gym, after the game,
I witnessed fire in the streets.
My head set on fire in Cambridge,
England, in the Whim Café.
After I applied Substance and Procedure
and Statements of Facts
my head was heavy, was earth.
Now years have passed since I came
to the city of great fame.
The same sun glows gray on two new rivers.
Tears I want do not come.
I remain many different people
whose families populate half Detroit;
I hate the racket of the machines,
the oven's heat, curse
bossmen behind their backs.
I hear the inmates' collective murmur
in the jail on Beaubien Street.
I hear myself say, "What explains
the Bank of Lebanon's liquidity?"
think, "I too will declare
a doctrine upon whom the loss
of language must fall regardless
whether Wallace Stevens
understood senior indebtedness
in Greenwich Village in 1906."
One woman hears me in my sleep

plead the confusions of my dream.
I frequent the Café Dante, earn
my memories, repay my moods.
I am as good as my heart.
I am as good as the unemployed
who wait in long lines for money.

Joe Louis

On the occasion of his burial at Arlington Cemetery, April, 1981

golden gloves melt on the hot sands
& the vultures wait for the white glint
of teeth handling white sheets
to join their feast
the desert is hot
& they are thirsty for hallucinatory peyote juice
so they can soar above a dead man
& ride the silver cloud of his hope
to claim his afterworld
where the thrones are not taken in sickness & age

he is gone
he is their boy now
the cameras flash over and over
taking snatches of his life
papers thick with his handprints
blow on the streets
he is their boy now
a memory in the sewers of time
the great white hope of charity checks
extinct in the unchallenged sun
they mourn with the false mornings that preclude dawn
tears thin as smoke trickle from their mouths
the cameras flash

& the vultures quench their thirst on the blood of bombs
& the vultures do psychedelic acrobatics on
   Southwind windowsills
the vultures gloat frenzied acorns in their jaws
charmed by their murders
& the punching bag flesh of a King

the ceremony is ready
planes hustle from the broad face of forgotten wars
to shoot hurrahs into the sky
to shoot down stars

fireworks blast over an ocean of bones
trumpets play the circus of dignitaries
ropes barring his flock
look on out of cracked mirrors
we do not know him in this way—
without the zoot suit smiles
   & softness of cotton balls
Niger running gold thru our fingers . . .
we are amazed that we have so little
  & yet so much
we are amazed that we have so much
  & yet so little
that the gold of our teeth
cannot be held by our hands

he is their boy now
the American dream
on the mortal bier of peace
brown bomber of German jellyrolls
ole Missus rescued again from yankee pants
the trumpets blow round table forests into snowflakes
Arlington is honored
he is dead now

the ideal warrior is dead
buried among the dead who were always ghosts
now roses will grow out of the mute earth
choked with evil
now towers will stand a little longer
to shoot lethal ink at sheep

we do not bleat
when the river bends another way
to feed the land
Joe goes with us
to the secret places of manhood
laughing at all the delusion in a silver coin

Arlington is honored
her perfumes drift to the moon
her gates open like the jewel of the lotus
to receive our King into their bellies
we are not fooled by the false mourning of mockingbirds
or the hidden rituals of unhooded knights
the round table turns
the chips roll down to the chicken coop

we are not fooled by the vulture's mask of bloody petticoats
he meant so much more to us then
a carnival of fallen saints
& pond water on sloping chins
they see tragedies we do not see
except in the world he was born into
& when he said: "We will win because
            God is on our side"
we heard djimbes & keelboats
& maul hammers destroying the steel forest
more than the gold of gloves woven in sand
the ultimate fate of tanks

we will win because
water cannot be defeated
        because
a leaf trembles towards the sun
        because
the wind, impeded, howls
& one cannot kill the deadly glance
        of selflessness

he is their boy now
as his flesh to them was always
crisp brown American apple pie
we do not bleat
when the river bends another way
to feed the land

for us he lives
as the sea lives
in the gentle rain of warriors breaking rocks
for us he lives in the strength of a corn seed
for us he lives in the silent wind catching snakes.

Calling All Brothers

*"And the male children were deaf to the pleas
of the mothers, and they couldn't see no men
nowhere they had to respect."*

Calling all brothers!
Calling all brothers!
Calling you out
from the hushed kingdoms
of corporate comfort;
calling you out
of your Mercedes and
your made-in-America commitment.
Calling you out of your cognac bottles.
Calling all my brothers
to break out of
your laid-off/unemployed blues,
break out of your videohypnosis;
calling all brothers, precious
as you are to your women,
cherished as you are by your sisters,
calling you out of your daze
of disgust with the family who sustains you—
your mothers, your sisters, your own brothers.

Calling you now
to *call off* your

"I ain't got no money, no job, no power"
dead-end trip. We see your anguish and
we understand.

Calling you now—nevertheless—
to the defense
of *your own life.*
Calling you to defend
your sons and daughters,
calling you to the defense of
humanity.

Dear Brothers, I'm calling you
to rise in the vacuum where
our African fathers used to stand
resolute against American madness.
I'm calling you to
take a position against children
with uzis and no daddies,
calling you to show the children
what uzis are for.

Calling you to a Great Reawakening
of African Fatherhood!
Calling you to form the ranks of
your own army—
your own army—
to take the streets from the babies
so they can grow to manhood.
Calling you to dare
the babies to go on dealing drugs over
your dead body!

This is our war,
a war holier than the Eagle

ever called you to fight.
This is our Vietnam, our South Africa
our Grenada, our Nicaragua,
in the streets of Motown, Philly, New York, LA—
on your block in our 'hood.

Calling you to dare
the monster death dealers who hustle the children
to face you down.

Calling all brothers,
crying for brothers,
moanin' for a brother,
dying for a brother.
Ain't no brothers nowhere?
Calling the makers of babies
to become their saviours.

Faye Kicknosway

Detroit

what Cadillac saw
what is no longer
the river
having come up from
its name, and the fort
its site and buildings
drawn first and sent

as letter; and history rose
from it—five flags
—as heat
—July
—and each succeeding
from upper lakes

as did the *Griffon*
Bloody Run, the whipping
post, Simmons

singing a hymn before
his hanging
a grandstand
of people come
to watch—a harvest

the throat makes, and Cadillac

his boot soles

—no waste oil wet them
or his breeches, no garbage, sludge
chemicals—he—this

timbered place
no curb to sit on
or scratch up
from

—the Corridor
and artists come: Luchs
Goodman, Newton, Sestok, Foust
—this earthly paradise

and swans
and quail and woodcock
and turkeys killed
thirty at one shot
—not oil captured
as twenty thousand ducks
one kill
in winter ice

this temperate
and fertile country, these

pleasure boats
and sailing vessels, these
sandy shoals
and deep currents, first
named Fort
Pontchartrain; and pears

brought to it
by two women

their small boat; and
fifteen thousand fish
in five hauls
a single seine; this

length of wheels
and charming meadows
and islands
and chiefly plum
and apple trees, this

heat
and thriving place
this straits, for bathing
and for drinking—and ladies

and children, the warm, clean
water—these fleshy banks
and fern
and cattails; ah

this earthly paradise
of North America

Margo LaGattuta

Alone in America

I am fourteen and take the Woodward Avenue
bus to shop at downtown Hudson's. I count
my money, one-hundred-fifty-six dollars
and twenty-three cents. I am amazed and
proud to be all grown-up, like a fresh
avocado, ripe and ready for anything.

I could be anywhere this 12th of December,
1956, in Cairo or New Guinea, but I am here
on a Detroit bus by myself, a teen with hormones
that surge like Greyhounds through my radiant veins.

The bus driver eyes me like a hungry snake, as I
pull up my straight khaki skirt to board. I imagine
he is Jimmy Dean and misunderstood. I want to rebel
and drive a wild Porche like Jimmy did, but I am now
becoming a young lady with white gloves and a veiled
pill box hat. I can buy my parents anything with this
pile of money in my alligator bag.

Money and wheels—the combination makes me shiver.
I'm so proud to be alive and alone in America, and
the riots in the streets won't start for years.

Oliver LaGrone

I Heard the Byrd

It was a bash!
It was a smash!
It was a blast . . . !
I heard the Byrd.
Memory came in
To help recall again
By image and by word:
Said my old friend,
"The fame is in the name" . . .
Broken reverie of a silver bell—
The muted trumpet casts its spell—
Rubdown with a velvet glove
And
Gabriel's blast from heaven above
All the way to edge of hell . . .

It was a flight of wings . . .
Names and birds again . . .
They called one
The Lone Eagle—
Name for a name . . .
Another, The Yard Bird.
And now a third—
The Byrd I only lately
Saw and heard—
Together,

Took me up by myself
With thousands on a sky-hi trip
Left us on a Shaky shelf
Then shook it!

Shook it!
Shook the ship to make us flip . . .
And dropped us with the sharp git-pick
Paced with bass and freted snare
And notes—
Ivory's melodic rhymes to everywhere . . .

Blue, black-white and silver-gold
All stations where the many-souled
Drawn into family of just one care . . .
To join the beat,
To keep the sound
Made by the "Bird's" appointed rounds . . .
No time or aim for mass conclusion—
Flight was the magic call,
The "Bird-time's" music fusion . . .

Fly on, Bird,
fly on!
The fame is in the name . . .
I heard the Bird.

To Rosa Lee Parks

Quiet brown woman,
Stepchild
Of the old Confederacy,
Shaking its rusty cradle

Deep in the land of your birth,
Stirring the graves of Davis and Lee
To change old Dixie lullabies
Into a song of human worth,
Into a song that grew to be
(As steel to the wills
of you and me):
That we ride as men,
Or walk and be free . . .

Quiet brown woman
From the new Montgomery,
Taking the path from
Her seamstress day,
Out forever
From the slave-bound way
(Till he took up the call
To lead in the fray)
To build an army,
A marching throng.
No sword or gun, no
Fife or drum—
An army with only
A marching song:
We shall overcome . . .
We shall overcome . . .

Bard of Hastings Street Bar

The man,
He looks like a nutnik.
When he presses me
Down in

The rutnik
While high
In the sky
A new moon sails by,
A mutnik
Aloft in a Sputnik.

Christine Lahey

Afterglow

Written after seeing Tales of Ordinary Madness, *based on*
Charles Bukowski

"That movie made me awfully thirsty,"
   you say, and I gasp at your bullhead-
      edness: you cannot understand why
         the prostitute closed up her womb
            with a giant safety pin. Some dumb
               Catholic hangup about chastity, you say,
                  (Turn words into poems, stick
                    them in prayer books, read them
                      like holy cards for indulgence.)
                        I crawl across Canfield, bloodying
                          my knees on broken wine bottles,
                            the bums' gunk of alleyways.

So ordinary to be mad. "Do they always
   drive crazy like this in Detroit?" he asks.
      And the child says, "Don't leave me alone
         in the house. I can't *be* by myself."
            Send him back to the barrio—he hasn't
               got a green card, or they'll find it
                  in the now too-well-known Korean Sea.
                     Not to worry. We're all *striding*
                      toward infirmity. Just drink up
                        and get on with it. "The coffee's
                       strong to keep you good."

•◆•

Motor City Men

for Kurt, Doug and Neil

Thank God
there are still young men
who wear biker jackets
and straight-legged jeans
and drag down Telegraph
to Base Line Eight
in Motor City.

Young men
who still live at home
or above funeral homes
Delray-way or by the Bridge
or in Lithuania-Town
who work in tool-and-die
or on the line
for nine bucks an hour
and fly at lunchtime
on beer and the big H.

Young men
who still touch children
and the right kind of women,
who are healthy as cats
and whose nails are dirty
because they still know
how to fix their own cars,
whose hips are small
under rolled-up T-shirts
because they don't dine
on gourmet food and wine.

Young men
whose hair is still wild
in braids long as Samson's
whose flaming beards
mark them metro prophets
who watch and wait
and gaze intensely
these thin young men
in Detroit City.

Michael Lauchlan

Elephants

At the deserted assembly plant,
on the siding that once led
to dealerships in Chicago, they wait
in boxcars painted for Barnum & Bailey.
By the electric fence, long unplugged,
we shift tired kids, wondering,
on the last warm night of a murderous summer,
why we've kept them out
in a crowd of lapsed jugglers
and laid-off welders, all
hungry for the indestructible elephants.

After the slow carting of cats,
the inexorable creeping of trains,
a door cries, sliding open.
Trunks sniff at ramps
and a head pushes into the yellow light
of the empty car lot.
Down the ramps they avalanche,
trumpeting and quavering, until circled by handlers.
They butt heads, link trunk to tail,
and move.

Outside the fence, kids flying past,
we strain to match their pace.
When they rumble onto the brick and asphalt

of Michigan Avenue lit violet at midnight,
the fastest kids stop just
an arm's length from massive legs.
One's trunk rips a weed from a curbstone
and stuffs it down, not slowing
as, past the bulletproof donut shop
and roofless warehouse,
we chase our sudden parade.

Liturgy on Trumbull

In midbaptism we rush from the house
to ask them to stop.
They had chased a man to the middle of this street
and were beating him.
Now he slumps near the curb while they name his crime.
I know Ronnie, the chubby guy with no shirt.
He lands one last kick on the thief's dazed face,
then backs off, cursing him loudly, demanding his "stuff."
"Go home for chrissake," his wife yells,
"or the cops'll take you." He leaves.

Ronnie's wife keeps a hand on the guy's shirt collar,
though he never even looks up,
just leans forward now and then to spit.

Someone lights a cigarette for the thief
while we talk about the city going to hell.
On someone's radio the Tigers are winning a ballgame.

My wife crosses the street holding a napkin.
For the life of me I can't think what she's carrying.
"Body of Christ," she says.

Fallen

His brutalized trunk lay quiet
stretched over the empty lot
embedded in frozen
grass felled by a chain saw
maybe city workers
looked like
he cut a wide swath
through the stinking air
buildings nearby
probably *shook.*

Parts of his skin
in snow
branches becoming soft
limp leaves dying
brown cringing
in the chilled night.

How long had he stood
Majestic leaves like
medals
reflecting the sky way
up above these crumbling
rooftops
commanding the birds
erect solid much

older and nobler
than this rotting city?

He lay there
silent in humiliation
fallen sentinel, general
critically wounded
refusing to call
for help indignant
deserving a hero's
funeral instead feeling
the black creep over
his softening skin.

He whispered to me
when I stopped & noticed & listened
and he asked me
to write this.

Philip Levine

The New World

A man roams the streets with a basket
of freestone peaches hollering, "Peaches,
peaches, yellow freestone peaches for sale."

My grandfather in his prime could outshout
the Tigers of Wrath or the factory whistles
along the river. Hamtramck hungered

for yellow freestone peaches, downriver
wakened from a dream of work, Zug Island danced
into the bright day glad to be alive.

Full figured women in their negligees
streamed into the streets from the dark doorways
to demand in Polish or Armenian

the ripened offerings of this new world.
Josepf Prisckulnick out of Dubrovica
to Detroit by way of Ellis Island

raised himself regally to his full height
of five feet two and transacted until
the fruit was gone into those eager hands.

Thus would there be a letter sent across

an ocean and a continent and thus
would Sadie waken to the news of wealth

without limit in the bright and distant land
and thus bags were packed and she set sail
for America. Some of this is true.

The women were gaunt. All day the kids dug
in the back lots searching for anything.
The place was Russia with another name.

Joe was five feet two. Dubrovica burned
to gray ashes the west wind carried off,
then Rovno went, then the Dneiper turned to dust.

We sat around the table telling lies
while the late light filled an empty glass.
Bread, onions, the smell of burning butter,

small white potatoes we shared with no one
because the hour was wrong, the guest was late,
and this was Michigan in 1928.

Photography 2

Across the road from Ford's a Mrs. Strempek
planted tulip bulbs and irises even though
the remnants of winter were still hanging on
in gray speckled mounds. Smoking at all times
she would kneel, bare-legged, on the hard ground
and half-smile when I passed coming or going
as she worked her trowel back and forth for hours
making a stubborn hole and when that

was done making another.
　　　　　When Charles Sheeler
came to Dearborn to take his famous photographs
of the great Rouge plant he caught some workers,
tiny little men, at a distance, dwarfed
under the weight of the tools they thought
they commanded. When they got too close
he left them out of focus, gray lumps with white
wild eyes. Mainly he was interested in
the way space got divided or how light
changed nothing.
　　　　　　　　　　　Nowhere does Mrs. Strempek
show up in all the records of that year,
nor do the few pale tulips and irises
that bloomed in the yard of her rented house
long gone to fire. For the first time I was
in love that spring and would walk the long mile
from the bus stop knowing it was useless,
at my feet the rutted tracks the trucks made,
still half frozen. Ahead the slag heaps
burning at all hours, and the great stacks
blackening the sky, and nothing in between.

Salt and Oil

Three young men in dirty work clothes
on their way home or to a bar
in the late morning. This is not
a photograph, it is a moment
in the daily life of the world,
a moment that will pass into
the unwritten biography
of your city or my city

unless it is frozen in the fine print
of our eyes. I turn away
to read the morning paper and lose
the words. I go into the streets
for an hour or more, walking slowly
for even a man of my age. I buy
an apple but do not eat it.
The old woman who sells it remarks
on its texture and tartness, she
laughs and the veins of her cheeks brown.
I stare into the river while time
refuses to move. Meanwhile the three
begin to fade, giving up
their names and voices, their auras
of smoke and grease, their acrid bouquets.
We shall name one to preserve him,
we shall name him *Salt*, the tall blond
whose wrists hurt, who is holding back
something, curses or tears, and shaking
out the exhaustion, his blue eyes
swollen with sleeplessness, his words
blasted on the horn of his breath.
We could go into the cathedral
of his boyhood and recapture
the voices that were his, we could
reclaim him from the brink of fire,
but then we would lose the other,
the one we call *Oil*, for Oil
broods in the tiny crevices
between then and now, Oil survives
in the locked archives of the clock.
His one letter proclaims, "My Dear
president, I would rather not . . . "
One arm draped across the back
of Salt, his mouth wide with laughter,

the black hair blurring the forehead,
he extends his right hand, open
and filthy to take rusted chains,
frozen bearings, the scarred hands
of strangers, there is nothing
he will not take. These two are not
brothers, the one tall and solemn,
the long Slavic nose, the pale eyes,
the puffed mouth offended by the press
of traffic, while the twin is glad
to be with us on this late morning
in paradise. If you asked him,
"Do you calm the roiling waters?"
he would smile and shake his great head,
unsure of your meaning. If you asked
the sources of his glee he would shrug
his thick shoulders and roll his eyes
upward to where the turning leaves
take the wind, and the gray city birds
dart toward their prey, and flat clouds
pencil their obscure testaments
on the air. For a moment
the energy that makes them who
they are shatters the noon's light
into our eyes, and when we see
again they are gone and the street
is quiet, the day passing into
evening, and this is autumn
in the present year. "The third man,"
you ask, "who was the third man
in the photograph?" There is no
photograph, no mystery,
only Salt and Oil
in the daily round of the world,
three young men in dirty work clothes

on their way under a halo
of torn clouds and famished city birds.
There is smoke and grease, there is
the wrist's exhaustion, there is laughter,
there is the letter seized in the clock
and the apple's tang, the river
sliding along its banks, darker
now than the sky descending
a last time to scatter its diamonds
into these black waters that contain
the day that passed, the night to come.

M. L. Liebler

Save the Frescoes That Are Us

for Edith Parker-Kerouac

These murals would have existed here,
in Detroit, even if Diego had never painted
Them. The sweat and labor of this city,
Along with the sacrificed blood
Of its workers, would have stained
These walls. No matter what.

This town, beautiful, lonely child
Broken by too much post-industrial
Hard luck, is always, once again,
Resurrected with deep convictions.
Our longevity cuts deeper than forever;
It's far longer than Rivera's Lenin-headed
Mural-Rock Center-Manhattan, torn
Down by those city slicker liberals in NYC
Beachhead of American culture and civilization.

Not here! The politics of Detroit
Go beyond arguing fresco vs. classic,
Or any something vs. anything. Here we deal
In a culture of collective energies,
Beating union heart. Here, it's always
Work–Not talk. We know that
Talk is cheap, but work is

Forever. We know
That building is more
Essential to our survival than politics
Is to our reality.

Mass Production

When we look closely inside
The tunnel of the American
Factory, we see gears turning
In disorienting prophecy, it is not
Salvation that first catches our eye.

Diego Rivera said "Industry is
Our Salvation!" What he dreamed
Was a much different nightmare
Of wires and gears and smoke-
Stack lightening than the burning sleep
Deep within the cavernous factories
Of our broken hearts where we are left hollow,
And alone on a cold highway
Of separation and pressing discrimination.

The American spirit has long been
Strangled at some untraceable point
Between the ideal and the real. Now,
We are hungry and we are waiting
For our justice to pass through
This system of mass production. The wheels
Grind slowly in a world of industrial darkness
Where the murderous dollar suffocates
Our hope with progress, and where
Our dreams twist in fitful sleep.

Our futures lie stricken in
Inanimate blankness as we wait
And wait, like our ancestors did,
for a change that surely moves
As slow as blood through the thick
Grease heart of oil fed machines.

Straw Boss Dream

Hidden within the center
Of the industrial crush
Of oil, metal bearing shavings—
The American Dream.
Drowned, breathless, stomped
Into hopelessness, strangled anger
The boiling pot of liberty blackened
By the greedy heart of elitism
And power. From a straw boss
Dream, we work to escape
The factory nightmares of lonesomeness.
Workers' souls are cathedrals
For harboring bruised labor, broken
Hearts and endless malaise. Alone
Our fear is work
Not "fear itself." Democracies
Are open market prisons
Where we all sell ourselves
Out to those who would
Otherwise rob us blind.

Naomi Long Madgett

City Nights

for Gertrude and Eddie

My windows and doors are barred
against the intrusion of thieves.
The neighbors' dogs howl in pain
at the screech of sirens.
There is nothing you can tell me
about the city
I do not know.

On the front porch it is cool and quiet
after the high-pitched panic passes.
The windows across the street gleam
in the dark.
There is a faint suggestion of moon shadow
above the golden street light.
The grandchildren are asleep upstairs
and we are happy for their presence.

The conversation comes around to Grampa Henry
thrown into the Detroit River by an Indian woman
seeking to save him from the sinking ship.
(Or was he the one who was the African prince
employed to oversee the chained slave-cargo,
preventing their rebellion, and for reward
set free?)

The family will never settle it; somebody lost
the history they had so carefully preserved.

Insurance rates are soaring.
It is not safe to walk the streets at night.
The news reports keep telling us the things
they need to say: The case
is hopeless.

But the front porch is cool and quiet.
The neighbors are dark and warm.
The grandchildren are upstairs dreaming
and we are happy for their presence.

Grand Circus Park

Twenty Years Later

Old men still drowse on gray park benches
watching a dubious sun leak through
the dying branches of elms.
    "The axe shall be laid (Hew, hew!)
    to the root of the trees . . . "
It is hard to realize
they are not the same old men,
grizzled and bleary-eyed as memories.

Bold, raucous pigeons flaunt themselves
before the glazed, glaucomic stares.
Young mothers quickly look away, caress
with special tenderness their infants' proper curls.
    "and every tree that bringeth not forth
    good fruit . . . "

The Cadillac bus still stops at the same spot,
but the passengers are not the same
and the point of exit is no longer home.
Even the wind is dying, and an autumn fog
settles like a shroud upon the old men's shoulders.
Do they dream of sputtering logs
in open fireplaces,
or do they shake with the impotent rage of trees
"hewn down and cast into the fire"?

Good News

for Leonard

The headlines never say good morning any more.
Every day the forecast reads: A chance of showers.
The Tigers keep losing the ballgames
And Dick Tracy is reported missing,
His smashed wrist-radio recovered
From a burned-out crater of the moon.
The market has plunged again;
Clad dimes and quarters have replaced the real ones.

But you ring the doorbell with a Sunday sunrise
Rolled up casually in one pocket
And a handful of silver coins
With rare mint-marks in the other.

The Street Life

We are the man downtown
with packets of dust
  enchantments of childhood
realized
  then lost too soon.

We are the crippled
panhandling
  measuring compassion
  in a tattered hat.

We are the woman
beaten by her man
Taste the blood in our mouth.

We are the skinhead
cruising for comfort
in the caress of chains.

We are the gang fight
the shakedown
the offer made by a runaway
to the driver of the car.

We are the love song
from the mouth of a 45.

We are the street life
the tyger and the lamb,
we are the ones who wait
beyond the open gate.

Peter Markus

Breakdown

Near the crest of the I-75 Rouge River Bridge
my car—a '74 Comet I stole off my granddad
for a dull penny and pint of Old Crow—coughs
then coasts to a stop on the side of the road.
I trip the hood, grope about blindly in the dark
while the engine ticks off its sputtering heartbeat.
After a while I shrug, "Fuck it," let the hood
drop, lean back inside and punch on the hazards.
I kick back on the busted bumper, wait for help
that won't ever come. Trucks muscle by in blurs
of dirt. I flip them all the bird, start footing it
home, though I'm five, six miles away. Below,
Zug Island smolders, a stump cut forest of steel
scorched by fire, a city slowly burning with rust.

Seven A.M., when I finally reach home, the sun
resurrects itself out of the Detroit River, turns West
Jefferson Ave into an urban mirage of underwater
concrete. Downriver, in the slag-rubbled fringe
of Great Lakes Steel, I find my mother waiting
alone in the still-night of her kitchen. Outside,
a lone porch lamp bleeds a halogen of metallic
light, causing moths to fly drugged into burning
glass. Silently my mother spoons black molasses
into her morning cup of coffee. She doesn't want
to hear about what happened tonight. It's enough

to see I'm alive and hungry. But my father knows
breakdowns cost. Not even the half-pint of whiskey
hiding in my coat pocket could ever make him forget.

Five/Eight Time

Neon jazzmasters gigging after midnight
in the Dizzy Gillespie dark,
time out, take five
with dapper Dave Brubeck.
Yeah,
smooooth.
And I was just a kid,
my old man slapping sides
on the turntable,
vinyl slabs weeping, moaning,
scatting alongside Ella Fitzgerald.
The cruel diamond,
in the groove of petroleum,
chrome monsters on the streets,
digging into the pavement,
jigging and jiving
up and down Woodward, Telegraph,
the long, lazy horns
wailing, wailing
in syncopation to dashboard jazz,
the jazz,
the jazz that swayed the
hips of a generation,
that holy Thelonius Monk,
the cold and lonely Miles Davis,

all of them, all of them
just laying back
and taking time
further
out
man, that's devout,
such holy sounds!

In Praise of the Natural Flowing

Out of the storm pipe, between the old path
& the unsold lots, the water journeys
at will this winter, flowing & floating
over its sheathing of ice: I see the clear riffles
angling & falling seaward; the continents
forming & formed, where ice, mud,
weed stuff & human discards run aground;
the channels & shallows forced between continents;
the reed clumps hummocked & footed like trees
with silt & debris; & down through the water
a fragile mud-tissue holding, half-shielding
the dead mingled leaves & the fragments of weeds,
like wing stuff in amber; the reed stalks prone,
combed out like the hairs of a long-drowned beast;
& the powdery silt & the clear openings in silt
where the water has winnowed its earth: I see
beside the water the gradual shelvings
of ice, contoured like land, reaching out
from its shorings & ending; & over the still places
the frail film ice, transparent as cirrus
or the membranes which form over the unborn:

I see in this world the natural flowing,
older than Genesis, slower than clouds
but faster than stone, which forms the rivers,

the lowlands & channels & continents of earth:
which feeds on life & tends ever towards life:

& I praise it, in gratitude & bitterness, knowing
this flow, vulnerable & beautiful, is permitted
to be this winter, between the worn path
& the scrawny stakes with the flapping red plastic
which claim this world.

Things Ain't What They Used to Be

Get them in their faces
Put them in their places
Tell the time by changes
Tell the stories less memories go blind
And all the emblazoned trails
In Detroit meadows are overgrown.
No vestige of valley paradise,
Black bottoms up, skirtail poppin' and Young.
Swingin' to some yellow knob stomps
Young and zooty
Come whistlin' through the succulent neck bones
Of a new prosperity
Swingin' with Hi-De-Ho hipness
Of the new jazztime swingin' city blues.
The big bad behemoths of FoMoCo
Stamped out the noisy money
Of five dollars a daily bread
Fed straightenin' comb doos
And piano dreams of ascension
From the crust of '32's stale cornbread,
There poured from hot metal crucibles
The forgings of a city of peoples
Of living dreams fleshed out of the hard temperings
Hard as the Joe Louis fist that bombed the intransigence,
Changing 'tudes, infusing the city with glorious promise
Lightenin' up the blues.

In a quest to make the freedom real
There were dreams spelled out in the policy
of lucky numbers
In the quest to make the freedom real
Free from deprivation and grinding sacrifice
Free from the maelstrom din of mass production's
Impersonal, implacable demands.

II

The Union sat down hard at the keyboard graphics
Of Black and White playing themes of solidarity,
Striking sparks of Flint and steel
To exact from the grinding servitude
Some measure of air and light,
Sparking revolutions that lit the horizon
With portentous auroras
Charging the smoking atmosphere
Empowering the Young men's voices
With sermons of outrage
Summoning gumption and resolve for the coming trials,
Passing the torch of courage and strength
To nourish the next generation.
Loose titty bustin' out on the Crosstown streetcar line
Nursed the young warriors that squelched
The flames of Holocaust
And cooked the goose steppers to a turn,
To a return to gin and smooches,
And nylon stockings,
And big ass slacks
And broken lives, and brokered dreams
Of restricted covenant ghettos,
Broken heads and broken hearts in the turbulence of change.

III

Ossian, Paul, Martin, Malcolm, Coleman
All came out of a legacy of resistance
Trying to make the freedom real
Young, a three button ace of a dude, Young . . .
One of the cats . . . a tyglon,
A erudite, irascible, obstreperous race man
Whose mouth could say anything
And say it like the jazz music he loved.
Bred from the fast black streets of the "hood"
Through war and circumstance made keloids
On naked feelings from battles with closed doors
Systematically slammed.
It came to pass he ruled the meadows
And fallow fields of fellowmen abandoned
To the pheasant, quail, creature refugees that fled from
The corrupted forests of the outskirts,
Young, man who was the proud helmsman of a rising
New city, redeeming itself,
Freshening with new promise.
Yet we profit from the life of one that rose so high
In the pantheon of the hip.

Ken Mikolowski

January in Detroit

Or Search For Tomorrow Starring Ken & Ann

I think it is interesting
though not exactly amusing
how we go from day to day
with no money. How do we
do it, friends ask, suspecting
we really have some stash
stacked away somewhere.
But we certainly do not
and we also do not know
how we do it either.
You sure are lucky,
some of our friends say. I am
none too sure of that though,
as I wait for the winning
lottery numbers to be announced
on CKLW. Thursday in Detroit
is the day of dreams. We have
been dreaming of a place
in the country lately and I'm
none too sure that is very healthy.
And speaking of health that's
also been a problem that probably
has something to do with no money,
since we've all been sick lately,

taking turns politely of course.
Could you bring me some more
tea one of us will ask,
and the other will.
In between the coughing and
worrying our thoughts
have often turned to crime.
We seriously wonder how we can
get away with a bundle with
as little risk as possible.
Last week we took our last
$12 out of the bank
and noticed how much more
they had there though
we had none. Of course
we wouldn't rob that bank,
they know us there
as the ones who bring
the rolls of pennies in.
And just yesterday they
fish-eyed us for trying
to cash our son's xmas bond
from his grandparents
after only one month.
So we wouldn't try to rob that bank,
but I do know of one up north
that may be possible . . .
I know this just seems like
romantic dreaming
but I practically make a career
of reading detective stories,
and God knows, I have no other.
Anyway if the right opportunity
comes along, we are more
than ready to meet it.

But this is a time of waiting, the
I Ching says, though it does
not say how we are to eat
while waiting. And soon
we will have another mouth to feed—
Ann now in her seventh month,
and that is often in our thoughts.
Besides all that we are both
over thirty, artist and poet,
still waiting to cross the great water.
Meanwhile, day after day,
there is still Detroit
to be dealt with—a small pond
says our friend Snee.
Big fish we used to answer him,
but that was a while back.
Now we think maybe Lake Erie
is the great water referred to
in the I Ching, and if we wait
long enough we can
walk across—to Buffalo
or Cleveland. In a healthy person,
says the philosopher, self-pity
can be a forerunner to action:
once the problem is seen clearly,
a solution may be found at hand.
And as I said, I think it is interesting
though not exactly amusing.

The Trans-Siberian Express

There should have been a warning on the door.
Buildings on the move, all over, everywhere.
They had loose tarps for walls
just being built, like sailboats heading
maybe for the river. Others made of gingerbread,
not heading anywhere
the wrecking ball just down the street.
For practice, firemen lit fires in the parking lots
laughing while civilians jumped
before they put them out.
No place was really safe. Imagination
comes with hazards. Thieves got in by kicking
down the doors. Got out the window,
through the alley to the street while cops
stood guns drawn in the hall. That never happened.
Late at night out in the hallway
all of us agreed. We never talked about
the loneliness, just
other neighbors. Next thing I knew I was leaving
after what had seemed like so much time.
And still I fumble with my keys, unable to remember
which one fits the door.

If I could only take a picture
everything would stay just like
it was. If there was laundry on the floor, or

toothpaste on the corner of the sink
that worked. I thought that things had
lives. They'd want to be appreciated.
The place was small.
I could have managed it. My
visitors would comment on the coziness,
but leave me for the night with
vague obligatory claims. Persistent
memory might reveal itself in
composition, but the presence that has
left the room and now sits warming
up the engine of her car across the street?
Some things you don't want on paper.

So much of what was there was not.
The upstairs neighbor practiced opera.
I had met her several times, not so nice
as drinking coffee with the windows
open in the spring while she sang.
Things need people. People probably don't
need things. They keep moving. Beyond
the wall next to my bed I heard a woman
throwing up each morning for the first eight months.
She left and the guy who took her place
threw up each morning, but a little
later. Winter came again. The furnace
shut off automatically at ten. The opera
singer shut her window and began piano
lessons. Practice for her often meant
the same notes played in repetition. I
began to feel as if I was the only one who
noticed time had stopped.

A delivery driver dropped his hat once. Through
the window you could see the brick wall of the

printing plant next door, and for a while you could
also see the hat there in the mud.
The place was on the ground
floor. To find out anything it wanted
all the street would have to do was
look right in. Then again, there
wasn't much to hide. Nothing really
happened there. One New Year's Eve I
scrubbed the floors and left. There might have
been a few dents in the walls. Before I drove
away, the furniture I had put out was gone.
Sometimes all there was for entertainment
was the traffic light. When it would change
so would the street, from red to green, and
so forth. Things could change. They
didn't need a reason. The light was
just a clue. So could people. That's
another story. I would learn that later,
mostly. Looking back.

Mary Minock

Down by the Boulevard Dock

A Poem for the Detroit River

Whitman could not have sung you justice
nor can I
river misnamed a river
more a braid
of ocean lakes
weaving gray ribbons and releasing them
into Erie's dark conformity

where old black ladies
and my old white mama
fish off the dock
and never catch anything,
but ask each other
"Catching anything?"

and watch the cast of water currents
and paper cups tell destiny
and are comforted—
old age the knot that ties the braid.

Down here at the foot of the Boulevard
I gaze against the wind upriver:
the bridge to Canada and freedom—
the skyscrapers against afternoon sun—

I rejoice in them and coke spills on the concrete
the cans, bottles, glass, permanent
concrete benches, aimed toward insight—
the river shall make us love
the course of our folly.

I see the dock
backwards in my experience
my father's hand to hold me back
before the concrete was poured,
brown cedar pylons sunk in the current;
a big boy jumps from the shore
and scales it;
we are open-mouthed—
certain death undertow—
my father's hand grasps tighter;

and then another time the lights at night—
the sign on the bridge flashes
"Ambassador"
and I twine with the boy
in the parked car—
white street lights, the breeze and sound of lapping—
I am pregnant this night
with the smell of the water on me—
a remarkable baby girl
full of oceans and fish that won't be caught will follow.

Now I hold the children's hands tightly,
the boy must go too near the water
drags me shivering
to where the concrete drops
"What is an undertow?"
wiggling the toes in his sandals

and so I pull him back to sit
on the bench where we lick good humors;
the freighters drag heavy
the mail boat rides high
and he is silent until he vows his life
to invent a river cleaner.

When Aunt Edith died,
we got her black piano
hoisted on a trailer and we rested here—
so drunk we played out-of-tune blues
to the wind;
the river caught the offering,
and wove the sonic thread into acceptance;
the piano purified
now stays a new generation
of undisciplined musicians
blowing hot and cold
who will not practice.

Today the wind picks up at sundown;
fishermen retreat,
the lovers are due,
odd children, mine among them,
connected to fishermen and lovers,
run through indestructible grass
planted over homogenized ruins
of a warehouse;
the old john built like a temple from the twenties
stands but is padlocked
and the drinking fountain
fails to work.

●◆●

The Wild Flowers of Detroit

Old gap-toothed whiskered one
look at you:
what front can front streets now put on
with these holes that show the alleys?

Close your mouth,
lest these lots show
your inevitable brick-strewn
wood-rot muffler-twist cement-crack
bent-wheel alimentary progress.

Don't cry, old woman,
we will sing some songs
and in singing them we will remember:

Here was a house
where a man and a woman marked their first time
and children smelled oilcloth
through the coming of the radio
the going of the coal furnace
the cutting of the elm trees

and they sat on the porch
late into the night
with the streetlight behind
the breeze-rocking boughs
to wait for the carriers
to shudder down this street
with canvas draped around their cargo:
and in the morning they would tell
fish tales of fins and tails
on the newborn models.

Here was a time when the busses ran everywhere
and the library stayed open
and the Irish stayed put
and the Jews claimed Dexter
and the Polish edged their lawns
and the first hard workers
who were black but might as well have been
red white and blue
scrubbed their children
edged their lawns
dressed up to go downtown
and tried to sing the tunes
together with your older children
who were jealous.

Here was a time when we almost got it right:
when the radios played at every stoplight
and cutting across the privacy of cars
and separate wanting
were words we all knew how to sing.
We bounced at our steering wheels
to the rhythm and the rocking
and gave your name to the music.

And here was the time
when your older children left
forgetting, not speaking,
to hoard the words to the oldest songs
like money
and so in August
we sing you to sleep
without the German lullabies
and with the rappers' radios
to pierce the night.

Old one of troubled sleep
who forgets her history:
you want to gather all your children round,
the gone ones the dead ones
the Mariachis and the gospel singers
and the vanished Delrey Gypsies.

Say you will not die,
until you cycle round:
when you will stop waiting
for the City to come with its mower
to cut the weeds that will show
the scalp patched with trash
that even your strong fingers
cannot scrub clean,

you will wait for Cadillac
who is maneuvering
the turn from the blue Huron
into the strait of green water.

He is coming this way.
He will land near what will be the Fort
and he will hack his way
through these bark-cracking vine-wood lots
to gather the wild raisins
to pick the wild flowers
cueiller les fleurs sauvages
to pick the wild flowers of Detroit.

Christine Monhollen

Solstice

Beyond this tree moss gathers
fully with reason creeping
by request specified through words
stretched far and over a horizon, thin
rivers quiet among these moments
held in unbroken curiosity
solid transformation of a 6 x 9 ruler
line accepted and centered
by the wanting eye.

It is not that art stumbles too long
or the thunder filling this head
frightens me as much as the automatic
sequence of morning following midnight
or the ivory bone conformed
as fingers justified as thumbs pushed
into the brain aside from the daily
buttoned blouse, the hat removed.

Beyond this hour the eye teaches
the color of significant waiting
the dignified canvas divided
by itself in contrast the hand tapping
out a backdrop condensed
into signatures carried in three chambers

as newsprint, an enemy of the present
bold with spacing ever diminished
ever flourished in the wounds of time.

Wardell Montgomery, Jr.

Roses Are Red

"Roses are red
Violets are blue
I am a poet
And so are you"

He said to me, "What do you think of that, Mr. Poet?"
I said, "That's a novel beginning, where are you going with it?"
"That's it man," he said, "It is a quatrain, two simple couplets of verse
A quatrain inspired by Coltrane while riding the F Train to Harlem
Do you get my train of thought?"

I said, "Your quatrain is too simple and not original
You've never been to New York
And the F Train goes to Queens. You are about the only poet
Who could listen to Coltrane and come up with something that
      weak"

He said, "There you go with your critique, Mr. Poet,
Criticizing my masterpiece. I don't have to go to your
Coffee Houses, Poetry Bars, Church Clubs
College Conferences, Workshops and Poetry Festivals
To read and write poetry that nobody listens to or understands

I don't want to visualize vague villanelles
Analyze any alliterations, be sensitive to a sonnet
Or sentimental over some silly sestina

Or believe a boring ballad by a bootlicking bard

I'd rather hiccup than haiku, free base than free verse
I am most skeptic about an endless epic
And I'd rather miss the muse than miss the news

Real poets are in the streets, in the shelters, in the ghettos
They get in trouble, they get high, they steal cars
They take what they want, they don't wait for an equal opportunity
They don't curse in verse, they curse the police at the very least
They live on the edge, they jump off the ledge
They don't send e-mail, they get drunk and go to jail
And you, Mr. Poet, won't even post my bail"

I said, "How can I cut you some slack when you never pay me back"
He said, "You can leave now, I am upset with you"
I said, "OK, here comes the warden and you upset me too
But I care about you
And before this chatter gets any worse
I will leave you with this light verse:

Dandelions are yellow
Lilies are white
Next time you are in jail
I won't visit, I'll just write"

Jessica Care Moore

Black Coals with Diamond Hearts

for Charlotte/Lyn/Tra/Angie/Alexis/Nikki/and
all my Detroit dogs.

What will they name us?
after we lie our bodies across the East and West Side divide
that swerves with motown myth and low ride grips down 7 miles
of nowhere to go streets

Gotta get my degree my car my house my man
my life together
but today I gotta bury him again
pretend I don't know them friends
moms wants to know why nice girls pin up Michigan's Most Wanted
on the fridge under the yellow butterfly magnets

Match the curtains   Match the description

We've dented car hoods with imaginary high heels
during Piston playoffs our daddy's play golf
Bad Boys were good ole days
Sometimes pissing outside was o.k.
The apple jack used to slip down with ignorant ice
Rolling after-hour red dice with somebody else's money
Suicide ruins the joy rides of drive by blood smeared
On our front porches
We simply keep brothas alive   silent sexy torches

Blowing fire into existence inhaling bullet proof wind
Ready for verbal war or a country cuss word
World news calls us a ghost town still I walk among old eyes
Pouring southern comfort on truck stop pancakes
                              that play numbers
Sixties riots still burn down homes in 1999
boarded up ashes, fire and black bottom dreams
committed suicide a long time ago
I see Malcolm walking down Woodward
Martin in Hart Plaza
And they don't recognize this chocolate city anymore
I've watched tears crawl back into our eye sockets
Without any time to cry we pray this time we won't die
when the club lets out
holding long kisses wishing we could
tongue down any man who's gentle
Or recognizes the feminine underneath the *westside* hat
somehow see my 7 Mile switch as graceful
never say goodbye to my cousin Lynn
smiling back black spirit child
got African drums under her white feet
strong heart screams lit up 24 hour Coney Island parking lot
your sicilian french blood was safe with me
I could protect you because I was down with the
          brothas from the Eastside who drove monte carlos with
tinted windows
Or an Impala with a 350 engine
we built in the backyard

Almost took you and Nikki out with ego-crushed bullets
Entering at close range through the driver's side window
This is a night out for nice girls with chicken-winged
Wishbones in their pockets
Ringing out dirty water from grounded clouds that fog our forever
Burning night smoke out of love sick lungs

Washing our feet with homegirl holy water
Store owners speak Arabic in our ears that smell of green meat and
    month old
bread repackaged and resold to our intelligence
Sticking bright neon orange three-for-a-dollar signs on our heads
Another one of my boys is shot dead
For stealing a five-cent tangy taffy
We are lawyers, journalists, business executives, poets, philosophers,
    activists,
hypocrites and confused
Intelligent hoodlums who hide dime bags in sweat socks
High off of the scent of new shoes cadillac cars and
Men who dress better than we do
Conscience of everything
Believers in fast-paced dreams
We Detroit, We Sistas, We Rosa, We Protest, We Laugh,
We Belle Isle, We Supreme, We Wonder, We Smokey,
We Booty Shaking Music, We Mid-West flavor, We country
We lay face down on warm cement
Pretending not to run after buses
Waving our transfers in the air hoping they will take us
Where we think we've always wanted to go
Detroit girls wait for the black sunrising
To turn young hot coals back to diamonds

Jan Mordenski

In the Sixties, They Banned Fireworks at Edgewater Park

but then, there, who needed fireworks?
Like lit-up candy necklaces, or glow-in-the-dark
rosaries like they sold in Woolworths,
rings of big round lights glittered off
the Tilt-a-Whirl, the Octopus, the Matterhorn
and the Midway. White lights followed
the rickety dip and curve of the roller coaster
that leaned toward the Rouge. And 'round towards
that stand of bandy trees, strings of lights
rode the steamy breezes of July over the heads
of dancers who, lightly touching down
on a plankwood floor, drifted to and fro
to the Platters and Pat Boone.
Out towards the parking lot, blue-white lights
stood in uniform rows, buzzing like big metallic
junebugs, bearing witness to the whines
of greasers and their girls, the promises
over fumbled car keys and phone numbers
mumbled in the dark. Even beyond the lot,
back beyond the river that
ran through the city like the leak
from a leaky hose, lights flashed
up against the night, tiny fireflies
dancing in the grass, riding up among the trees,

floating, seemingly, like midnight dreams,
like memorized prayers, like tiny stars
given back to the night.

Like Colavito

Believe me when I tell you nobody but an
eight-year-old girl could mourn so much
the trading of handsome Harvey Kuenn that spring
but change was in the air in a city that
negotiated its way into and through the Sixties.
"Tiger" Stadium just made sense, named for a team,
not an owner, that has always operated more on loyalty
than on pennant pinching and cash (though HE
was a good fielder, too). So up from Cleveland
came the dark horse, the feisty fighter.
who was murder with a mitt and loyalties
transferred, as noiselessly as a handful of salted
peanuts from my Dad's pocket to his leathery hand
to my tiny palm, wet and pink and drawn from the
leather pocket of my own fielder's glove.
It was a casual thing. Though Indian fans
rampaged for years, citing that one little trade
as the downfall of their team, here in Detroit
we took it in stride. We were building
a reputation, a rock-solid loyalty that would go
beyond bleacher seats and concrete walks. Colavito
suited us then—hard-spitting, hard-hitting, yet so
noncommittal for most of the game. Like Colavito
we would be cool, collected, until the pitch
or the rotten call and then we'd come out slugging.
No, he was no gentleman, but, as I said,
things were changing, and nobody knew that better

that year than an eight-year-old poised on the
right-field line, bundled up against the winds
in a little Am. League jacket who, dusting the salt
from the wounds of her hands, waited, crouched forward,
stretching out her glove to catch whatever time
was going to toss her.

Edward Morin

Facing Away from Detroit

and toward the wet horizon
I bob two minnows from a cane pole
to fake the wavery swim of hundreds
that cluster nearby in lapping water.
A herring the size of my forearm surfaces
and disperses the school bellies up.

Sooner or later a beauty will strike.
My son in scarf and parka
and a baseball cap with earflaps
looks ready for a moonshot.
He bobs his pole in sync with mine.

The herring's mouth is small and tender,
the pull from April water steep.
You have to hoist one steadily overhead
and fling it back onto the concrete.
Otherwise, herring loosen from the hook
and drop back into safe water.

No fish has bitten.
Yet. One soon will.
That's why our situation now is perfect.

Ted Nagy

Beneath the Grand Heaven

Beneath the grand heaven
vanished tools of youth break
mechanically, maniacally
through shattered walls of clouds
—of staid visions

. . . and there I was,
walking wet rains through torrid excitement
my umbrella packed neatly in the trunk of my mind
—my head, dripping with knowledge onto bound pages
stretched with simplicity
—my city, lunged forth with reality, desirous and tender
with rage, the secret rage of squalor and excellence
that inertia and ignorance cannot teach
—the puddles ring circles beneath towering tenements
crumbling
—city buses cut steam into tiny squares . . .

i've seen the city spit,
open mouthed wide with diesel teeth,
grinding factories of smoky soot,
lips that scrape skies and bleed concrete rains . . .
i've told them all a hundred times,
it's all on the outside: go . . .

my dream is insane conversations,

passion that i have never known . . . until now.
on side streets beneath the bulk of city lights,
cold tremors warm as the snow rests gently on branches
of after school walks.
high tide renaissance, glassy in the distance . . .
hey buddy, my references are slow . . .
wake up cass and palmer and throw down the keys . . .
—my eyes, ultimately, a witness to canvas examination and
lyrical proliferance.

i mutter the city singing
raise a fist high to the moonbeams
but then again, as taxi cabs creep up from behind,
whittling rubber,
sloshing puddles,
naima crying . . .

(detroit's divinity lies honestly in essential minds,
the wounds pain and the smiles rise,
it's all naked beneath the heaven,
the bare bones of hell)

. . . and i walk along, taut,
steamed and screaming jefferson avenue—the species,
lingered there is terra rubble,
walking on subjects of advocation . . .
—and when i see the ragged bums scavenge through
the clothes in my car, i sense the beauty of lostness,
and the gain of knowing ignorance

. . . and so i opened the book
and the closed mind
kinked its neck

Strait City

strait city
city of straits
Detroit
where straight people scream
in the green comfort of beer bottles
their eyes kooly smoking like menthols
from the straight edges of tables
Detroit
where strait pallets thickly long
for the crooked taste of white apples
and minds smolder in the beaming glare of silicone
Detroit
where children trapped in the shadowy straits of
dispossession
blink huge eyes
and silently scream:
> we need art
> > can't cry for it
> we need art
> > we die for it
Detroit
freak city
city of freaks
where reckless poets
taste blue apples
behind red doors of solitude

no strait city cast of freaks
for them
no cinematic supporters
tossing huge stares
or rotten tomatoes
in their reckless directions
Detroit
we need art
we cry for it
we need art
we die for it

The Father the Son and the Spirit

Reflections on Black Detroit

I. The Father Speaks

My children, How shall I speak to you now?
Shall I sing softly with soothing guitars that
question our masquerades?
Shall I speak loudly with rough thundering
flames that slay your children and drive
your men's minds mad with flaming desire for
ghostly whores?
Shall I fill your streets with wild slobbering
idiots, drunk with fear of the light, armed
with dark rage that threatens your elders?—
An' what of your elders?
Those whom my spirit has hovered over
and protected these long years, how shall
I speak to you of their suffering . . .
The time weary laughter that now sits
trembling before the loud danger of bar room
frenzies.
And what of your children? Your youth . . .
the tender offspring of Love and desire,
shivering with cold loneliness beneath summer
suns. My children, How shall I speak to you so

that you will hear and walk to the Light?
Walk to the Light . . . walk to the Light . . .

II. The Son

"The flowing radiance falls to the earth
burning and cracking the pavement
and a tiny green bud burst through
to smile upon a new day . . ."
My brothers I give you my very life.
My sweat I give you as we
dance shoulder to shoulder in house parties
and disco cabarets. My tears I give you
in the alleys of snowy winters where you
lay slain by the choking anguish
of unfulfilled dreams, bullets and wine
bottles, and pale demons that strangle.
My very blood I give you as it pours
from the wounds of our deaths as martyrs
in the cause of Freedom; from Southside
Chicago to Soweto township. I give you my
blood, the screaming remains of O.D.'ed
musicians, aborted babies, and mangled
factory workers;
ground and pulverized and spit out—their
substance dripping from life eating machines.
My brother, I give you my life—As a lamb
slain in due season. Eat of my flesh
be filled, grow strong, and fight on
till dawn . . .

III. The Spirit

"In the beginning was the Word"
Listen and you will hear

the song of victory dancing in the trees.
Listen, rise early, before the birth of
the sounds of the city, and listen you will
hear the soothing sound of victory dancing
with the beating of your heart. Listen make
still your soul and listen to the inner song.
It is the song of victory. The trees know it
when they shoot forth the first spring green
after barren winter. The tiny sparrow knows it
as the light of the day dawns through the fresh
cracks in his shell. The children of Vietnam
know as they savor the hard won prize of new
freedom. It is known in Zimbabwe. Hear the
marching feet.
It is the song of victory.
The song of Freedom
Uhuru
It is the spirit moving in
YOU

Kristin Palm

Motor City Trilogy

I

Everyone crashes
at some point in this city.
Often, we see it coming.
I watched my accident
in the rearview.
As with most things in life,
the apprehension
far outweighed the impact.

Relief came not
so much from the absence
of injury as the determination
that it was not my fault.
Still, I did not emerge
unscathed.

The car, after all,
had been totaled,
a passing
I could not take lightly.
She was my first.
She had a name.

The adjuster's assessment
rang in my ears
like the hideous crunch
of metal on metal:
Total loss.

Never mind
that I'd paid her off,
that I called her Marge.
Never mind
that she'd seen me through
four apartments, two jobs,
Amy's wedding,
Tecla's funeral.
total loss.

After the exodus of friends
bound for better positions,
my sister's move to the mountains,
my boyfriend's inevitable decision
to leave me for hockey,
after tenuously coming to terms
with all this newness under my skin,
how could anybody take away
this one, last familiar thing?

II

Her insides
felt so new, stiff,
foreign—an import, a sin
in this city, but all signs
pointed her way.

Our most reliable model,
the salesman said,
noting she was the last on the lot.
A wise investment,
my father said,
insisting he'll worry
less.

He called her Ruby
to ease the transition,
recognizing the importance
of a name, remembering
the Subaru he'd relinquished
20 years ago and only when
the floorboards wore through.

I sat for a while,
breathing her new car smell,
sterile and adult, calculating
interest rates, considering
options—alloy wheels, cruise
control, security. I keyed
the ignition haltingly,
drove off the lot
slowly, watching
my father
in the rear view,

shrinking.

III

There are days I own
this speeding,

sprawled-
out
mess,
drive the freeways
end to end
just to feel connected.

I don't need power
steering, power locks,
power windows, power
anything. I know
every Marathon station,
Taco Bell and 7–11
from Detroit to Calumet,
can keep myself fueled,
fed and caffeinated
clear across both peninsulas.
I've got Big Chief, Slot,
Thornetta on the tape deck,
the 16-valve thrill of acceleration,
5 speeds, a spare tire
a clear rearview and no sense
of direction.
I've got all the power
I need.

Other days it's too much,
this crazy, cramped culture,
zipping us down freeways
vital as veins, spindly things,
crisscrossing counties,
linking us in ways
we never touch. No standing
on the bus or squeezing
onto subways here—

Jesus, we rarely even walk
to the corner—
just 2.2 million half-ton
capsules cruising highways
as familiar as grandparents,
so integral we name them—
Fisher, Jeffries, Lodge—
memorize each pothole
and speed trap in pathetic attempts
to expedite commutes, reach
wherever we're going
to move on
to the next place
and the next,
always late and never
time to stay, damn
the traffic jam, construction,
anything that slows us down.

We curse
congestion, honk
and gesture, punch
up all-news,
all-sports, all-
oldies all-the-time, cut
each other off,
whatever we can do
to simulate control.

*It's 8 A.M. in the Motor City
and traffic is backed up for miles.*

We tune in WJR, WCSX,
WWJ, WJLB, WRIF, WHYT
with AAA and eyes in the sky,

traffic and weather together
up to the minute and on the :08's.

It's 5 P.M. in the Motor City
and traffic is backed up for miles.

We live fully equipped
and loaded:
A/C, CD and cell phone,
to make us feel at home;
ABS and all-wheel,
so we think that we can stop;
passive restraint and air bags —
NHTSA approved —
to keep us strapped
and cushioned
when we finally
hit the wall.

It's midnight in the Motor City
and traffic is backed up for miles.

Alternate routes are advised.

Ted Pearson

from The Blue Table

VI

rubble

the common lot
vacant

abandoned

where gathering
gathers talk

of the weather
talk of the town
and the streets

bordering
this desolated

stratum

unrelieved
weight

from above

from *Coulomb's Law*

IX

back streets parallel the main drag
empire tours   local tongue
a mental defective wins a job
there is no solution to this lyricism

XX

blue angels mock heroics
workers sun their ankles at lunch
narcosis of the deep   an indefinite article
sex in a four-wheel drift

XXXI

city limits sleep cycles   frayed nerves
versus metal fatigue   arpeggiated wonders
body and soul   the celebrated
pleasures of the mouth

XXXIV

brick window   glass house
neighborhoods tourists never see
the gesture is empty but what could fill it
tympanum   distant thunder

My Light

I don't have to give up the rhythm
in my blue light for bitter company.
The wings are mine, and when it's time
to leave, I'll leave.

Plenty of my stars
won't be any duller than
the glare from your dusty stage lights.
Take time to eek out
the bitter juice from every line,
so that none of it gets wasted in my drink.

And if that train tunnels down
our track shorn kisses,
I'll out the lights
of glowing Fisher building beacons
and wait in its shadow
for hunger and sweetness
to creep back in unnoticed
and scare me back my
electric light impulses.

Ode to a '64 Chrysler

Pearl White with a waterfall grill
left the assembly line in March 1963
rolled off onto Jefferson Avenue in
pre-riot Detroit, and was presented
to my grandfather on his retirement,
fifty years with the company, first
Hudson, DeSoto and finally Chrysler.
Veto Hugo Tremonti or Monty (as his
coworkers called him) used to pick up
my sister and me, with Hershey's chocolate
bars for the drive to Vassar where we'd
have grand Italian picnics in the park
with Polenta and meat sauce cooked in
black cast-iron pots over an open fire.
I went to my first funeral in that car
for a great uncle I'd never met. The
priest eulogized over his casket, laid
out in a khaki canvas tent in the
country, proclaiming that only those who
"believed" would see the promised land;
the rest would burn for eternity in hell,
I cried out, "I believe, I believe,"
amidst the silence. Later in my life,
Gramps used to take us to Belle Isle to
the aquariums and greenhouses, 'til he

was too old to drive and that car would
just sit in the red-and-white garage
behind his house. Every Wednesday when
I was over at his house for dinner, I
would go out back and look at it with its
push button automatic and sofa-like blue
plaid bench seats, until one day Grandpa
died of cancer in his 79th year and they
draped an American flag over his casket
for fighting in WWI at 17. I inherited
that two tons of American steel, 15,760
miles and 14 years old, I'd wash it every
day, steam-cleaned all 413 cubic inches
of that V-8 with a hemi-wedge block and
bendix four-barrel carb. I drove it
constantly and the next winter, was run
off the road and just missed a telephone
pole but brought it back on the road in
a spin hit a dry patch and flipped one
and half times it slid on its side to
a stop and I climbed straight up and
out the passenger door without a broken
window or a bent fender to be seen the
two truck driver hooked it up to his winch
pulled it back down to all four tires with
a bounce he stood there and scratched his
head at the huge mass of unharmed metal.

Ghosts of the Central Area: Detroit

Now the wreckers come slamming the brick walls away
  A chimney falls a kitchen crumbles
Wires assault the air slicing and quivering
  A home goes down to dust

One hundred years ago the proud owner and builder
  Stood side by side viewing it
"First home on a new street—brave start"
"Wife can hardly wait to get into that kitchen."

Through the doors the kids, the laughs, the dog
and years produced grown-ups who moved off to marry
  Parents grew old and passed away
The last clack of horses hooves erupted
  Now a new family in an aging house

Making repairs living passing in and out
  Now tears and sometimes shouts
Another generation now driving cars
  Followed by the rental owners
A once proud house sags windows no longer glisten

People come and go a lonely dog barks
  Shadows of past ghosts soar among streetlights
Nobody sees or notices a red light in the window

Cabs ease by the passing of men
A house still by day now sinister and alive by night

Renewal plans are made and then one day
A man with a brush and yellow paint comes by
    He X's all the houses on the block
Now the wreckers come slamming the brick walls away
    A chimney falls a kitchen crumbles
Wires assault the air slicing and quivering
Ghosts of the central area rise up
    And fly into eternity.

After Attending a Poetry Reading on February 14

In poetry as in the rackets
ya hafta hustle, be there, get seen;
as GM goes so goes the artist
and so I went . . .
Well, no sweets no stings
in last night's drone.
And—O I sat so straight—
certainly no love.

Look, once I sat in movies—
dim Saturdays in Saginaw,
the Avalon and war bonds in the lobby.
And Marilyn Trier. She'd lean against
my arm and slump. We'd neck . . .
Marilyn! At soft sixteen
what we discovered!
Christ!
And now I sit at readings. Straight.

Look, I want verse like teenage love
to find me in the dark, to feel
me up, touch and take
my touches back. And kiss
and sneak adventure in
and put me on the verge . . .
but all I got last night were words

pulled down by wires
made loud by boxes,
and all I did was sit. Too straight.

I'll send a card . . .

Dear valentine, come slump with me again.
In small-town Avalons we'll tempt the new.
Hell, I don't care if I slip down and dirty.
I long for hideout matinees with you.

Lines from a Highland Parker

> "At Chrysler headquarters in Highland Park,
> north of Detroit . . ."
> From The New Yorker, May 5, 1980, in an article on
> the automobile industry by Joseph Kraft.

North of Detroit? They do it every time
them city slickers. They have no goddamn sense
of true direction. "Oh, you going to Kansas?"
they will say. "Won't you stop and give regards
to my cousin in Milwaukee?" Such jerks.
And now here's me in Highland Park
a cinder's throw from the Chrysler complex
and Lynn Townsend Drive, and am I north? Am I now?
No suburb here; I'm surrounded by Detroit,
I'm in the center. I'm in a swivel chair
that spins. Things hold. Detroit
does not lurch out much, thanks I think to me.

And to the south, lands laid waste in '67,
old brick churches, and the Kresge mansion

future drug-cure center. And to the north
the movies, fuck-and-suckies, ladies free,
not to mention Ted's-On-The-Park,
the Greatest Little Restaurant in the Middle West.
And this is the beginning only. Cars slide up and down
on Woodward streamier than your New York taxis,
& small-claim stores with glassed-in clerks
speak a care Fifth Avenue would only dream of.
And broken bottles east and west. And a sign "Fillums
    Developed."
And a donut shop. And no pedestrians but cripples.

Highland Park north of Detroit? New Yorker, smug
    cosmopolite,
proofread thy soul. Your great white way already pales.
While far from that dimed marketplace folks like me, we
    radiate —
for who stays here is at the hub.
But slant the map to suit yourself; it's we who see the land.

Aaron Ibin Pori Pitts

An Epitah for Ogun in 16 Movementz

they played the drums
az it ushered forth the spirit
itz sound the very heartbeat of life itself
the very voice of the cosmik spirit
like the solo bazz speaking with the percussionist
speaking of the heartz
one listening to the other
az one—az other
ebony voicez they speak in tonguez
playing the instrumentz of life
we too drum/dance
acrozz the heavenz
in calling r ancestorz
their namez we beeeee calling
hearing their wailz/their whisperz
their singing the praise songz of r birthz
we beeee hearing their shouting of the field hollerz
where the bluez came forth that singz the improvisational
musik we now hear az jazz
but we really beeeeee speakin' in tonguez
of the visionz we've seen
visionz within the heartbeat
visionz of the land of ife
visionz and visionz
that some say that u beeeeez crazy

but then these visionz
r within their heartz and they beeeeeeez
scared to watch the visionz flash acrozzz the heavenz
scared to see them
to see their ancestorz beeeee calling
these visionz that u see
so painting on carz
nsibidi paintingz that interpret the heartbeatz
of ogun . . .

Sonya Marie Pouncy

Detroit Poem: Part One

I am your mother
I am your children
I am your city
I am your soul

I am sidewalks
where children play jacks
I am cracks that break
mothers' backs
I am the god of fire
burning down walls
shaping metal into guns
I am faygo red pop days
better made nights
and the wondrous bread of life
I am your brand new Cherokee
parked out front
minus radio and tires
sitting on blocks
I am dragon green with malice
soldering lives together
I am the stench
of life urinated
in downtown alleyways

I am your mother

I am rummaged garbage
that your old schoolmates eat
I am coal under pressure
becoming diamond cutting rock
I am cracked ground
steaming with anger
for the blood I've been
forced to swallow
I am folding chairs
of storefront churches
that have been packed
1000 times
& the salt of tears
that mourn edge park
I am monuments of buildings gutted—
a testament to human strength
I am the groping fingers of teenagers
searching for island pleasure
& the callused line workers' hands
driving on the river of life

I am your father

I am southern thoughts
of freedom & work
blazing paths to rivers edge
I am high time paris fashion
crippled by dutch elm disease
I am *fuck you motherfucker*
and *let jesus save your soul*
I am the glide in your slide
that says you must be wearin' 'gator
and your hair's got to be laid

I am broken spirit/battered womb tea
sipped with semen crackers
in corridor cafes
I am the womb
around which pylons gather
the archway to many places
& the packaged perfume
of blue collar sweat

I am your children

I am the blue light rhythm
of a hundred-ton press
I am the driveway
where your mother was killed
for the $3.75 she had in her purse
I am festivals of a thousand faces
that make the body dance
I am the belt that disciplines
noosed tight 'round a junkies arm
I am that fabled forest
become bottom bitch's reality
I am dandelion breaking concrete—
a flower whose nature is to bloom
I am amoeba symbiont
absorbing everything in my path
I am a black man's raised fist
displayed horizontal
but still a fist

I am your mother
I am your children
I am your city
I am your soul

Dudley Randall

Old Witherington

Old Witherington had drunk too much again.
The children changed their play and packed around him
To jeer his latest brawl. Their parents followed.

Prune black, with bloodshot eyes and one white tooth,
He tottered in the night with legs spread wide
Waving a hatchet. "Come on, come on," he piped,
"And I'll baptize these bricks with bloody kindling.
I may be old and drunk, but not afraid
To die. I've died before. A million times
I've died and gone to hell. I live in hell.
If I die now I die, and put an end
To all this loneliness. Nobody cares
Enough to even fight me now, except
This crazy bastard here."

            And with these words
He cursed the little children, cursed his neighbors,
Cursed his father, mother, and his wife,
Himself, and God, and all the rest of the world,
All but his grinning adversary, who, crouched,
Danced tenderly around him with a jag-toothed bottle,
As if the world compressed to one old man
Who was the sun, and he sole faithful planet.

●◆●

George

When I was a boy desiring the title of man
And toiling to earn it
In the inferno of the foundry knockout,
I watched and admired you working by my side,
As, goggled, with mask on your mouth and shoulders bright with
    sweat,
You mastered the monstrous, lumpish cylinder blocks,
And when they clotted the line and plunged to the floor
With force enough to tear your foot in two,
You calmly stepped aside.

One day when the line broke down and the blocks reared up
Groaning, grinding, and mounted like an ocean wave
And then rushed thundering down like an avalanche,
And we frantically dodged, then braced our heads together
To form an arch to lift and stack them,
You gave me your highest accolade:
You said: "You not afraid of sweat. You strong as a mule."

Now, here, in the hospital,
In a ward where old men wait to die,
You sit, and watch time go by.
You cannot read the books I bring, not even
Those that are only picture books,
As you sit among the senile wrecks,
The psychopaths, the incontinent.

One day when you fell from your chair and stared at the air
With the look of fright which sight of death inspires,
I lifted you like a cylinder block, and said,
"Don't be afraid
Of a little fall, for you'll be here
A long time yet, because you're strong as a mule."

● ◆ ●

Bag Woman

for Jane Hale Morgan

Wearing an overcoat in August heat,
Shawls and scarves, a torn and dirty dress,
Newspaper shoes, she squats in the Greyhound terminal
And rummages through two bags, her lifetime treasure.

She mines wastebaskets for her food and clothes,
Forages in the streets with sparrows, pigeons—
Isolate, with fewer friends than beggars have—
another stray cat or abandoned dog,
she sleeps where cats and dogs sleep, in the streets.

Sister, once did you suck your mother's milk,
And laugh as she fondled you? Did Daddy
Call you his Dumpling, Baby Girl, his Princess?
And did you flirt with him, bending your head,
And, giggling, kiss his eyes through your long lashes?
Did some boy love you once, and hold you tight,
And hotly know you through a summer night?

Or were you gang-raped, violated early,
And from that trauma drifted down to this?
Or, born defective, abandoned to the streets?

Sister, I do not know. But I know that I am you.
I touch your rags, clasp your dumb eyes,
Talk with you, and drink your fetid breath.

Jon Randall

DE-troit Summerscene

when summerstink crawls the street on its belly,
& heat sings itself in black skin—
when sad stores sweat flies and watermelons,
& tarbaby whores melt on griddle beds—
then dangerous young men rule the corners,
razors & tension in their pockets—
they burn in the streets like coals,
& DE-troit, burnin, fries a busted yolk of sun—

Kevin Rashid

An Invitation

What would it take to have you come here?
What would it take to show you
how I pull, each day, the gauze from memory
to mourn with your Telkaif,
to weep with my D'Jdaidet,
to uncover the wordless pact we made here,
in this city, where our moms and bobs came
like everyone, on their way to some other place—
a site, this Detroit, used like the cars that killed it
to get to Maryland, San Diego, that house
the other side of Eight Mile.

Yet something held us,
something beyond our parents' corner stores,
behind the out-bound expressway—
memory, that wild, incredible infant of passion
we promised to raise from its dark-wood contours,
that divey saloon . . .

Now here I am, Master Inquisitor,
frantic archaeologist,
scrambling to piece you together.
Now, everything has fallen to the ask and the answer,
to lousy fiction with several endings
to survive its purposes.

What would it take to have you come around
and haunt with me the dead forests of this city—
Where Ishmael was nowhere to be found
and Hagar, herself, was on the verge
of leaving a good thing alone.

Historical

I look west, down Merrick—
the sun fallen away
beneath layers of reds, oranges, purples, greys,
the vision through a smog-lensed sky,
the factorial West—
how those colors call back
another vanishing point—
how as a child I'd haunt
museum versions of older Detroits
where time falls back
down a single street
from the cinema to the druggist,
the five and dime and the firehouse,
the cobbler, the blacksmith,
the stable, the press—
falls back past the Fort and Cadillac
to the silhouette peaks of a picket fence
broken and weathered
like the soft ends of driftwood,
surges and echoes
into those hand-painted, back lit
tears of color
and how it felt precious and flirted
and promised something past it
and the song of my failed allegiance,

my false apology—
falls back on nothing that cares,
nothing that needs,
no one who waits.
How my street, Merrick,
empties into the West,
echoes the memory
of a museum.

Marilynn Rashid

Zena

He comes to many doors
asking the same question, "Zena here?"
Everyone is surprised to see him on their porches,
a large imposing man with long dreadlocks,
his clothes tattered, rank, becoming earth.
No one knows Zena, but he is suspicious
and comes back several times before convinced.

He has been here twice
and now I find he's coming to my brother's house
several blocks away, past the projects
on the other side of the freeway.
"Zena here?" "No Zena here."
"Is that a quote?" he asks my brother.
"No, that's the truth," my brother tells him.
but he's been back again, and yet again.

My day locked in, how rarely I waver,
I know my place, my house, the numbers that complete me.
But he asks me and I begin to wonder—
where are they now,
lost, absent, dead, fallen from our certain grasp?
Not here I tell myself. Not here,
we tell each other.
Is that a quote?

Shooting at No One

I get up in the middle of the night
to make a list on a page
to write out of my head
the things yet to do
the letters to write, people
to call, the bank, the bills.

And when I reach the page's end, I hear
a freighter bellow low and loud,
a long clear moaning, so close
it seems the river has jumped north
to Forest Avenue.
Then gunshots—
one two pause, one two three four,
with quick even spaces in between.

Who is it pointed at? Who's pointing
the gun? I picture the scene
in a nearby alley before I can
stop my head.
Then, no, I slow my panic,
forming another solitary drama,
something that might help me sleep again.

A lone man on a high porch
shooting at no one to empty the thing,
shooting into the air
that's all, to empty the thing
into the air,
empty, the air.

Eugene B. Redmond

Aerolingual Poet of Prey

> *for Alvin Aubert who surveys Life from the quiet's deep see.*

Through a two-way telescope of time,
he tracked the stormy calms of history.
Carried gravity in his sight. Behind
him stretched a flapping scroll of ir-
reconcilable callings. Before, there
swirled a grinning turret of racial
daggers aiming to splinter the brother-
ing father within him. From goober dust
rain lore graphite red beans gut-trails
creole-dreams ink river korean-conflict
mardi-gras typewriter bible nightmare
ritual-rice and computer he forged wings
of discovery/wings of delivery. Gained
griot-height. And, orbiting, gave birth
to *Obsidian.*

Became poet of prey:
South Louisiana aero-linguist. Resur-
rected life's raw incenses. Reforged
cool word bolts. Moved North: leaned
South. Kept *Feeling Through.* Kept com-
ing smack up *Against the Blues.* Kept
planting earth harp in air.
       In-flight, he drank his brew

of laments: *trouble-deep rivers*
river-deep troubles

In-flight, *skimmed fear off death.*

Poet of prey:
Scavenger who claimed and climbed language.
Rocked and groaned through love's highlow.
Closed: Opened in the moontime of need. Follow-
ed quick/eccentric dartings. Entered slow/blood-
filled hiding places. Lusted after sizzling carry-
overs. Twitched in the rumble-quiet: In the
sweat time of riots. Watched the glitter of
upheaval grow sheenless in the logic of
darklight. Wrote. Wished. Salivated. Stayed
Case. Stayed edge. Stayed course.

Poet of prey:
Proper poppa chronicler. Lured concentric
florals of grief into slim sleeves of poetry.
Into rural sheaths of jubilant anger: Into
lyrics of coiled, knowledgeable passion.
Into folk-lucid tropes. Holy-evil. Grimace. Twist.

Poet of prey:
Hear his sober ecstasies resonate. See
them levitate midst the heart's acoustics.
Alvin Aubert: clear, spicy, bright babble
made edible as in a gulp of blues. Inhalable
like the first pungent breeze of gumbo.

Detroit Circa 1989/90

my 14-year-old niece debra
    (now a big time engineer in texas)
was a shining scholar
at renaissance high school
when she took me shopping
    (twice in one day/
    late morning & late evening)
saying uncle gene some detroit malls
change colors between daylight & night

so you gotta see this soular shift
from joggers, leisure ladies & retirees
to boom/boxed lovers, gold-magg'd bmw's,
concentric-chained brothers,
statuesque nubians in leather frocks
& beepers emblazoning boyz 2 men

& at the cine each theater has two shows
    (one on the screen & one in the audience)
so you need a rubber neck for 360 degree
        spectacles

detroit's got lots of window shoppers,
uncle, some with their own country
operating on their own time

Scrapyards: Eastside Detroit

Sometimes you might find yourself driving
through these neighborhoods of blocked-off streets
that are never accurately rendered on city maps,
and always you discover that wherever you are going
you can't get there through here, and always
you notice among the ruined neighborhoods
and closed business structures making their defeated gestures
along the unkempt avenues the prospering scrap-metal shops.

Huge trucks pass in and out of these sand- or slate-colored buildings,
and in the yards that you can see there are stacks of squashed car
    bodies
or piles of metal sinks like cast-off crustacean shells.
What seem to be the petrified wings of butterflies is torn-down
    siding.
Rusted metal pipes are the pulled-out veins of cardiac giants.

Once these neighborhoods were filled with first generation families,
fathers walking to church in panama hats, holding their wives' left
    arms
in their right arms, the women's black shawls hanging down to their
    waists.
Once there were small mom-and-pop shops on almost every
    corner—
bakeries with old-country bread, butcher shops with raw meat
    hanging

from iron hooks.
Peddlers and knife-grinders walked through the neighborhoods
and old men bent over under sacks asking for rags.

The immigrants left an iron life to settle on the city's margin
and build their lives out of leftovers, out of taking what nobody
    wanted
and making it valuable again through hard and humble work.
Where have their dreams gone? Did they pass through here to their
    true destinations?
Were any of them still here when the business of reclamation began,
the scrapyards spreading into the crumbling neighborhoods?

The scrapyards are their monuments, admitting through their gates
the masses of cast-offs others regard as junk
into the democracy of waste, where they dream of the fires
that will transform them into marvels of utility and grace.

Leslie Reese

I Love You (The Heidelberg Project)

for Tyree Guyton

I love you
I know the workings seem obtuse
in this rubble glitter sanctuary
you portrait my face like doll's
my knees burnt by pavement and
eye-blinking teeth-missing kids
blooming
heartflowers from a window box of
thundering polka-dots
& new psalms scripted in the *queen anne's lace*

your face is peeling off the
side of the house
flying like kites sucking penny candy kickball
mining memory banks
with the dull ends of abandonment
spotted and dotted by your tender blinks and tiddlywinks
numbering my love letters loud:
like a dixieland horn section
blazing a tear of trust in the house to obstruct the just

dream phases you send me through
dripping deep pink sky
wailing sirens forever in the

                haunted house of
motown metallica chug mouth industrial exhaust

               I can't seem to
          peel that crust off, that rust
               like whitewash
        or the cornstarch our children
       will come to crave the crunch of
         rust and mildew and faded grins

letting your question marks be the divining rod
      through the history of my body of
          big white teeth and GOD
                  GOD
                  GOD

     spinning our urban weather vane and
                 trapped
e it. I know I am hanging right side up in your tree brain
          tricycling spine-tickling
      mustachioed. brilliantly resilient. shaming
        cowardice heads and eyeless traitors
oo my shoes with rain and nostalgia. I gotta be moving on.
at time o'clock shall we hoist and caravan our suitcases?

Rod Reinhart

Detroit 1983: I Am Waiting

I am waiting for the bridge to be built
Ravens wrangle overhead as it rises from the water
Picket signs protest the majestic imitation of architecture
Expressways melt like the Wicked Witch of the West
Ships with rolled steel
Set sail for Saginaw
Alligators touch my tongue and smile
As I wait for this bridge to be built

I am waiting for this bread line to end
Snowflakes swirl around me
Like a Wyeth Winter scene
I almost expect a cheery farmer
To tramp these blizzard streets
Seeking a flowing maple
Among this forest of the poor
Who would kill for a little syrup
To cover their spoiled cheese and day old bread
Who know in their hearts
They are but the Avant-garde
of freezing bread lines to come

I am waiting for the fires to go out
Twelfth Street and the Algiers Motel
Are garden memories
While the flames of '67 still rage in the eyes

Of those who never take their passports past Eight Mile
They sift the ashes of burnt-out slums
Like archaeologists, seeking evidence to sanctify their hate
As if riotous memories of ancient flame still touched them
Intimately and innocently as Gandhi
And burned their mother's ear

I am waiting for the war to begin
Waiting with this coffee and shish kabab
While students march with Reagan signs
And old men dance like Zorba in the streets
We are all skewered by missiles built on Texas plains
Millionaires clink beers with presidents
Widows huddle beneath palm trees
While babies shudder to the roar of military boots
Cameras roll and my coffee flows to ice
As I wait for the war to begin

Serious Childhood

My first memories are of walking a picket line.
Somewhere I sit on the steps of a downtown building.
I am very small.
We are singing Solidarity Forever. My mother
keeps me away from angels and Madonna pictures
and fears the nun's fervor in my eyes.
She is not Catholic.
Her big dare was to cross a picket line,
drop, secretly,
a stink bomb, perfect and round,
crushing in its paper bag.
The department store crowd
scattered and screamed
and she loved her braveness.
I still loved angels but thought
she was one.
She talked about freedom and dignity;
I saw a solitary riverside
where I turn myself into a mermaid.
My mother sang, "Just like a tree a-standing by the water,
we shall not be moved."
We were serious in those days.
She took me to see the Diego Rivera mural at the art museum,
car-factory workers full of sweat and muscle strain.

She said rich people didn't believe
working people worked that hard.
I look at the angel pictures.
We both meant it.

Michele Valerie Ronnick

Conditor Huius Urbis: A Triptych for
Mr. Woodward (1774–1827)

I. On Naming Myself Augustus, c. 1806

My parents named me Elias,
But I am Augustus now,
A founder of cities,
A Romulus reborn.
I'm making the map for a grand, new Detroit,

A city to last like Roma Aeterna,
Debricked and made marble by Augustus Caesar.
I dream a dream of a thriving metropolis,
A midwestern center, a queen of the lakes,
Propelled by wheel spokes of infinite rays.

II. Orange Seeds for Thomas Jefferson

The 12 I sent to you in April were just enough
To start a small grove, an orangerie
On top . . . of the hill . . . of your handsome home.

But eight weeks later you were dead,
'Though Adams thought you lived,
On top . . . of the hill . . . of your handsome home.

I, a youth, and you, a man,
As scholars, talked together,
Of stars and schools and capitol cities
On top . . . of the hill . . . of your handsome home.

Later, when my peninsular life
Was led at your discretion
And north and west, then south I moved,
I remained with you in heart and soul
On top . . . of the hill . . . of your handsome home.

III. *Epitaph for a Gravestone Lost*

Fifty some years were given to me,
And I lived them all very well.
Yet subsequent time has not been kind;
My sun has been eclipsed.
So stop right here! Read these words,
Since death awaits you too!

No wife—I never had children.
No likeness exists of my figure or face.
No stones point out my grave site.
These deeds are my only remains:

I led Detroit after the fire of '05 and through the war in '12.
I laid out her streets, encoded her laws, and opened the first lyceum.
I designed a place "for all human learning," older than Jefferson's
    school.
So remember me as I merit, for I was a founder, too.

In Tallahasse I died. In heaven I live.

Jazz/Blues/Jazz

Session at the Greystone

I was moved by the combo.
I felt it thru and thru.
I fell in love with the guitarist,
The saxophonist too
Fused together to become one body
One must understand and know.
Jazz/Blues   Jazz/Blues
That it starts from the first breath
That comes from the soul
feeling put to music.

Jazz/Blues   Jazz/Blues

Releasing explosive high notes,
low notes,
sweet notes penetrate the air,
no longer strangers, or frustrated hearts
but starts reconciling
each other with the clapping of hands.

Jazz/Blues   Jazz/Blues

Pat your feet, clap your hands,
Stand up! wiggle, cry a little!

The first spade for the foundation
has been laid!

Jazz/Blues   Jazz/Blues

It brings back memories of days
Long gone by.
Promises of tomorrow
Even though they are lies.

Jazz/Blues   Jazz/Blues

Unaware we live thru them all
the time
that no longer remains the question.

Jazz/Blues   Jazz/Blues are the guts of life.
The soul of a man.
The parable of the Black.

Jazz/Blues   Jazz/Blues.

Michael Ashton Rosemond

Mothering Birds

The rite on Cass and Temple

The birds come singing to her.
She throws seed from her second-story window
descending,
in dull clumps on early mornings when rain
stiffens bone and tendon;
in delicate spattering on good days,
when her arm is strong.

Chemise slipper footed,
she approaches softly.
A jeweled porcelain cat observes the morsels,
as it peers over verandah, sun and time,
glistening like a sequined dress.

The wind clings painted on her gown,
pressing breast and belly and thighs
with ageless hands touching,
ordaining her to pore over the birds.

In parks, in crying streets of cities,
in mineral alleyways,
from windows,
from hearts holding mystery;
they feed the birds—

these whom God supplies all
and who's sparrow's death does not escape
its bantam darkness from his sight;
are constrained to be fed from their hands.

the old women who are joined
around the orb, by mystic sinew and muscle;
fellowship daily,
disinterred from bed and morning,
to toss bread and seed,
in slow arcs mothering.

John Rybicki

Gravity

I swing the glass door out
to the cold monks on Warren Avenue
who bow toward me for change.
I hook left and take the sun
into my mouth, wanting to fight
a physical fight, swim toward her
through tar and die swimming.

The sky pulls itself
into me and sings, until mouths tear
open all over my body.

I can say the earth blows out its green,
and that seasons are the pace
of God's breathing;
that I take a bottle to my head
and not a gun; that I hold my mouth up
to people and move it like a sock puppet;
that shingles I snapped
from garage roofs still fly;
that she found the marbles I lost as a kid,
handed their power up to me and said,
This is how the world runs: swallow.

Osvaldo R. Sabino (translated by James Hoggard)

Chameleon Posing with a Passport

for Natu Poblet

She's a woman everyone notices.
She has no children and has traveled a lot
—But no one knows where she's been—
Sometimes she'll look poor,
But it's only one of her poses.
She has no name and never gives replies,
She changes character with the weather,
But that's also one of her poses.
No one knows anything about her background,
We only know she never had kids
And travels whenever she can.
She has chameleon-like outfits
And the only thing certain about her
Is her dark and carefully guarded passport.

Jacqueline Rae Rawlson Sanchez

Drew's Mom

Sunshine bright walked into
La Biblioteca Publica Bowen
March 11, 1998
wrapped in a former Duffield—
she's moving on—
BL package
and that's not bacon & lettuce
thank you much.

The tea drinking Aquarian granddaughter
is
a big-hearted,
soft-spoken
—don't underestimate her—
flute-playin', toe-tappin' bluegrass
cool jazz, add a tad of R & B
world & classical rhythms
music in her soul
woman,
but don't play her country!

La mujer con los ojos azules
claros como una laguna de agua limpia.
La mujer con una sonrisa that could melt
and most likely has melted many a cold heart.
La mujer raised in Wixom

when Wixom was just a small dot in the road,
is a culturally minded, community oriented
she means business
woman.

Trinidad Sánchez, Jr.

Why Am I So Brown?

for Raquel Guerrero

A question Chicanitas sometimes ask
while others wonder: why is the sky blue?
or the grass so green?

God made you brown, *mi'ja*,
color bronce — color of your *raza*, your people
connecting you to your *raíces*, your roots
your story/*historia*
as you begin moving towards your future.

God made you brown, *mi'ja*,
color bronce, beautiful, strong
reminding you of the goodness
de tu mamá, de tus abuelas, your grandmothers
y tus antespasados, your ancestors.

God made you brown, *mi'ja*,
to wear as a crown, for you are royalty, a princess
la raza nueva — the people of the sun
It is the color of Chicana women —
leaders/*madres* of Chicano warriors
luchando por la paz y la dignidad
de la justicia de la nación Aztlán!

God want you to understand . . . brown
is not a color . . . it is:
a state of being, a very human texture
alive and full of song, celebrating—
dancing to the new world
which is for everyone . . .

Finally, *Mi'ja*
God made you brown
because it is one of HER favorite colors!

Let Us Stop This Madness

> Derek Barfield brutally died—brutally died
> Clarence Scott brutally died—brutally died
> Chester Jackson brutally died—brutally died
> a hundred kids brutally died—brutally died
> brutally died, brutally died.
> S.O.S.A.D. (THE WAR ZONE)
> Errol Henderson

The bullets from the guns
that massacred the invalids
in San Miguel, El Salvador,
the bullets from the guns
that killed the poet
in Johannesburg, South Afrika,
the bullets from the guns
that kill the actors on TV,
for no other reason
than our own enjoyment,
are the same bullets
from the same guns

that kill the children
in Detroit, Michigan,
Chicago, Illinois, New York City,
Miami, Florida,
Los Angeles, California,
Austin, Texas, Houston, Texas,
San Antonio, Texas.
The bullets from the guns
that killed Martin Luther King, Jr.,
that killed Mahatma Gandhi,
that killed Bishop Oscar Romero,
are the same bullets
from the same guns
that kill the children
in Detroit, Michigan.
When will it stop?
When will we learn
to listen to the artist
teaching the children
songs of life,
songs of love,
songs of liberation?
Let the children
grow into man/womanhood.
Let us stop weeping
for the invalids in San Miguel,
for the poet in Johannesburg,
for the children in Detroit.
Let us take a stand.
Let us stop the bullets
from the guns
that kill our children.
Let us stop teaching
the children
that the bullets from the guns

are the only way
to deal with life.
Let us destroy the factories
that make the guns
that shoot the bullets
that kill our children.
Let us take a stand
to share life,
to break bread
to break bread
to break bread
with each other.
Let us stop this madness . . .
the bullets . . .
the guns!

> As one of his last acts, the day after
> Patrick Purdy machine-gunned five
> children to death and wounded dozens
> of others in Stockton, California,
> President Ronald Reagan
> pardoned a man convincted in Texas
> of illegally selling machine guns.
> by Lars-Erik Nelson, Tribune Media Services Inc.

Passion Fruit

In the rubble of the Vernor's plant
newly demolished, men
pick through bricks, and the late
bright sunlight finds a hole
in the standing wall, a hole the size
of the world. The pink bricks
clink and slip lankly into piles,
some for keeping tossed to the truck
where men stand in surplus store coats
beating their hands like boxers.
Two years ago Vernor's was an emblem
of the uniqueness of Detroit, Michigan,
its burn at the back of the throat.

Denise Sedman

Untitled

Get me out of this idea,
off this winding urban road,
this path of destruction
leads to a house
with gingham-checked curtains
a white picket fence—
where children smile, eat Slow Pokes,
wait for me at the gate.

Get me out of this idea
that I need to be a person
of substantial success
measured by things
no one really owns
anyway.

Material things, merely vacant accumulations—
A house becomes too small,
the diamond not big enough.
The idea is something you can grow into:
a moo-moo dress that fits twenty cows.

I want an idea that stays, lasts, grows,
mushrooms like the cloud of Hiroshima.

ii.

Get me out of this idea that America is just,
and capitalism rules the world,
better than socialism, communism, fascism.
America has the best government—
This huge idea constricts blood vessels in my brain,
stops me from thinking about new ways
to keep people on the streets of Detroit
from killing each other for a pair of overpriced sneakers.

Get me out of this idea that I can
make a difference in a world,
where I am a speck of dust
in a giant bowl called earth, a world larger
than I can imagine because my mind
is too limited by traditional thinking,
trapped in an orderly world,
church on Sunday, work from nine to five,
children to nourish until a clone emerges.
Duplicate ideas stand like corn in a row,
a perfectly plowed field,
thigh high by the fourth of July,
dominated by nature's laws.

iii.

Get me out of this idea that all men are created equal,
when Peruvian mountain women carry burdens
larger than they can balance, wear heavy weights

on their heads, move laundry to a blue stream,
wash daily grime from cotton covering brown bodies
in a different fashion than models on a Paris runway.

Get me out of this idea that I need a Calvin Klein suit
to wrap my curves in a way that says, "hire me,"
I'm a professional writer who wants a paycheck,
maybe some health insurance, to have my American pie,
George Washington cherries promise me truth,
America will feed me jubilant plumpness, ripe goo,
bullshit from Madison Avenue, Wall Street tycoons
want it all for themselves, and I just want a job.

Get me out of this idea that I can live off the land
like David Thoreau. I need Ralph Waldo Emerson
to take care of me, give me some acres on Walden Pond.
I don't look good in stripes—can't go to jail for not paying taxes.

Get me out of this idea that I can write poems,
beautiful sonnets like Shakespeare, words that last centuries,
through wars, famine, hatred—these words will not change.

DENISE SEDMAN   329

The Jonahs

Caught in the belly of denial
I sleep in the stomach of a fish
with broken dream catcher
wedged in my nose
acid bathing turning
in rotisserie hell
I pray to drown
it would be easier to suffocate liquid
water flooding like asthma

Caught in the float of a sputum
we choke and cough plasma
in this space of triple limbo
in this sleep of in between
in this belly of whales
where our faces reside
deep in the center of zero
vacant with the horror of empty

Caught in the wobble of membrane
we the alpha Amoebas
lost in the interpretation of allegory
we the regenerating tissue

Caught in the company of televisions
caught with the canned smile of media

Caught

UPSIDE DOWN
in West Mecca
IS BAD FOR THE BRAIN
in the involution of ayat and scripture
NEVER DRYING OUT
in the kidney of Detroit
FROM ALL OF THE RAIN

CAUGHT CAUGHT pressing auto parts
from our loins
caught looking into the mirror of emphysema
raiding the blue in the deep sea

Caught eating the striking pig
caught participating in new sport of
    Fish-throw-back
caught driving the interstate
through the blackest bottom

double caught talking to portraits of
initials MLK, JFK, yo G LMNOP

CAUGHT

in a 3rd dimensional laugh ha ha ha ha
caught with monkey breath
caught in a Sudanese factory
looking for a pharmaceutical
caught in the vulgarity of virus
         distribution
caught in the symbolism of beach bleeding
    (E. Coli wading area right this way)
Caught making love to a painting

(but oooh girl he looked so real)
Caught balancing a unicycle on the
    curved line of zero

Caught believing in the circle of powerlessness
caught dizzy in the sewer of religion
caught not listening to the mouth of a
    water glass—truth pouring like gravity
caught in the brain kiss of death
caught in the wind from a domestic slap
caught in the web of isms
    in the bramble of history
    in the branches of missing hands
caught in the rain
caught like a captured African
caught like a diabetic amputation
caught like a no winged bird
caught celebrating Christmas and High Blood pressure
caught climbing down a mountain
in the glue trap of rodents
caught in the rain

Dennis Shea

Random Beyond the Confidence Line on the First Day of School

It's easy being young
in drab egg-and-buscart George's place
where the food's pseudo-Greek
but the chiseling's pure.
Noisy laboratory for
sound students with muffs,
Is impossible to concentrate on Cicero here,
Is impossible to concentrate on Bob Talbert here.
The leg report on the weather guess
says no miniskirts till at least Thursday.
It's cool and leaves haven't fallen:
illegal now to smoke near piles of leaves
and soon a crime to pick one up.
Something against family values, bad sign
to the kids, who should
be zeroed on Fortran
and the How-To-Watch video,
to prepare for a life of staring.
Behind the window, students, walking
cheerful and fast
under knapsacks and supple eagerness:
I wonder only how
some go to school
in Detroit four years

And come out naive and clean-cut,
talking about their cars,
perceptions unsullied,
like unmeshed gears,
shiny and unused.

John Sinclair

the Screamers

for kenny schooner

stagger down overgrown sidewalks
of memory. giving hand &
giggling. earth angel, how I long

for you. where you been, all these
years. johnny ace, with a hole
in his head. where you gwine,

ivory joe? or those stupid white
imitations, the "crewcuts," jive pat
boone, stealing their songs. "sh-

boom." "two hearts." chuck berry,
jimmy reed. "i walk 47 miles
of barbwire. i use a cobra snake

for a necktie. i got a brand new house
by the roadside, made from
rattlesnake hide." o you really

really send me, baby, you
got to go for me or i'll
beat yo ass. who

do you love. (weird lullabies. "broken
hearts." long, long &
lonely nights. for your

precious love, I wd have drank
gasoline, & all i wanted
was a little water. where i came from,

mysterious ofays of the imagi-
nation. why you aren't here
with me, old gang, beer-

drinkers, bull-
shitters. where
did you go?

consequences

After John Coltrane

The music moves inside myself,
I mean I feel saxophones in-
side my meat, a force in-
spiring that meat
to sing pure electricity. Flashes. Scream,

move out from the wall
of yourself. Out from there,
Now, or you stay there. What you thought
that man was screaming, that he wanted
to get inside you. "You," again, like some stupid
broken record.

The music moves inside,
& stays there. A part of what you are. & NOT
"from". But the song of meat energy
burning to come through you. In charge. & that energy
makes its way. Yes, shapes it, & is in charge. *In,*
goddammit, IN the meat,
and *of* it. Yes,

yes, yes. A
firming it. & where you can go
to find that one place, I mean
it *is* the meat. And the song
that moves that self,
& shapes it, ah, ah,
       well yes it does.

Ella Singer

15th and Dalzelle Streets

at the corner of fifteenth and Dalzelle streets
stands the old union train station
now abandoned;
each shattered window
a broken dream
corinthian columns stand ancient graceful
flanking corridors no longer crowded
now dark
now dank
now dangerous
forgotten gates where dreams once met
and intersected
for a while . . .
tracks that lie alone desolate
now rotten
now rusty
now raggedy
broken bits of bottles
littering refusing to become one with earth
clinging like forgotten refuse
look like an unneeded time table . . .
the marble walls have become
the canvas of urban artists
the receptacle of poets prattle

abandoned building
standing mute
as a still life
waiting . . .

W. D. Snodgrass

Old Apple Trees

Like battered old mill hands, they stand in the orchard—
Like drunk legionnaires, heaving themselves up,
Lurching to attention. Not one of them wobbles
The same way as another. Uniforms won't fit them—
All those cramps, humps, bulges. Here, a limb's gone;
There, rain and corruption have eaten the whole core.
They've all grown too tall, too thick, or too something.
Like men bent too long over desks, engines, benches,
Or bent under mailsacks, under loss.
They've seen too much history and bad weather, grown
Around rocks, into high winds, diseases, grown
Too long to be willful, too long to be changed.

Oh, I could replant, bulldoze the lot,
Get nursery stock, all the latest ornamentals,
Make the whole place look like a suburb,
Each limb sleek as a teeny bopper's—pink
To the very crotch—each trunk smoothed, ideal
As the fantasy life of an adman.
We might just own the Arboreal Muscle Beach:
Each tree disguised as its neighbor. Or each disguised
As if not its neighbor—each doing its own thing
Like executive's children.

At least I could prune,
At least I should trim the dead wood; fill holes

Where rain collects and decay starts. Well, I should;
I should. There's a red squirrel nests here someplace.
I live in the hope of hearing one saw-whet owl.
Then, too, they're right about Spring. Bees hum
Through these branches like lascivious intentions. The white
Petals drift down, sift across the ground; this air's so rich
No man should come here except on a working pass;
No man should leave here without going to confession.
All Fall, apples nearly crack the boughs;
They hang here red as candles in the
White oncoming snow.

Tonight we'll drive down to the bad part of town
To the New Hungarian Bar or the Klub Polski,
To the Old Hellas where we'll eat the new spring lamb;
Drink good *mavrodaphne*, say, at the Laikon Bar,
Send drinks to the dancers, those meat cutters and laborers
Who move in their native dances, the archaic forms.
Maybe we'll still find our old crone selling chestnuts,
Whose toothless gums can spit out fifteen languages,
Who turns, there, late at night, in the center of the floor,
Her ancient dry hips wheeling their slow, slow *tsamikos*;
We'll stomp under the tables, whistle, we'll all hiss
Till even the belly dancer leaves, disgraced.

We'll drive back, lushed and vacant, in the first dawn;
Out of the light gray mists may rise our flowering
Orchard, the rough trunks holding their formations
Like elders of Colonus, the old men of Thebes
Tossing their white hair, almost whispering,

> Soon, each one of us will be taken
> By dark powers under this ground
> That drove us here, that warped us.
> Not one of us got it his own way.

Nothing like any one of us
Will be seen again, forever.
Each of us held some noble shape in mind.
It seemed better that we kept alive.

A *Woman Singing the Blues*
while Cleaning House in Detroit

Whenever I have to do the most ordinary things
I remember the great women, Ella, Besse Smith
singing their way through to fame.
Take this Detroit dust I grapple weekly
with lemon oil and bafflement—how it
brings back my friend's mother saying
the way it comes, its tub scum thickness,
is like nowhere else. Did not know why,
she always said, but it had to be
the river and the lake mixing themselves
up in the factory smoke.

As I use the sponge brush to lift cat hair
and dust from the surfaces
of couch and chair and throwrug,
I imagine if I were a biologist, I would study fur
why it stops growing at a certain length
and hair does not, what in a fur cell says *Enough!*
when my hair presses on and requires me
to go to the hairdresser whose conversation
is of flowers and how long it has taken the scientists
to find cures for cancer so many friends now have.
Even there, in the hairdresser's chair,
leaning back, head wet, Sinatra crooning forever
on the radio. I imagine if I were a composer,

I would write a coda to a symphony
with some new sound, like the held rhythms
of Mr. Blue Eyes, a bell with honey in its call,
anything at all to ring a small change that lasts.

I say, the days I make clean
the borders and surface of a life
that veers and teeters on a moving river,
disordered, tended, and unseen,
I often come on it, from behind, like this,
my own life, seeing it whole, in a moment,
like a river barge in a storm, or, more,
like driving on a Detroit city street,
full of green and rubble, and
hearing clear and private, in some
setback house in the trees,
a woman singing the blues
in full, and perfect voice.

Keith Carter Sterling

Detroit Grand Prix

Of course
there had first
been the metal
of the stamping plant,
the power
of its engines.
Before the cool steel
of the revolver.

Then the car driven
off course
his foot to the pedal
of the vehicle
left idling.

In his hand was a purse
to which his blood lines
added a splash of color
to the white interior
and the pavement.

There had been a woman
who shrieked
before streaking
from the scene
her engine racing

to the solace of the curb
crying.

It was at least an hour
before the EMS truck
arrived.

Someone had the good sense
to cut off the engine
as he heaved his last breath.

The metal in his mouth
open
from the bullet
matched
the steel grey of the vehicle.

He seemed prepared to sing
the chorus
of a blues song
or perhaps
some sad gospel melody.

The heat radiating
from his mouth
was a hiss of smoke
which matched the smokestacks
of incinerators
and factories now closed.

He had cursed her
one time too loudly
hit her
one time too much.

Pulling the revolver
from her purse
she had shot him
before running.
The handle of the gun
too hot to hold.

Across the street
the neon lights
of the bar
flashed
as figures danced.
Their mood swing
spotlighted
his assailant,
the only noticeable emotion.

Renée Tambeau

Renaissance

the waxing and waning of the moon
summer comes with longer days and later nightfall
afterwards, comes darkness
there is birth, harvest, and fallow
everything is cyclical
pheasants and geese are taking over the city
buildings have turned into gardens wild
what is organic comes to claim its own

an oil slick on my tongue
words slipping like gears
my speech tells stories of salt
mountains and mountains of salt
and this salt buries men
men who work for the salt to be worth their own
part of a machine, they go on working
and we go on ivy covering anything slow enough
to get in the way

in a city park turned hollow
there is a statue whispering
I held paradise in my hand and I lost it
moss is softening his mouth
but he whispers to the moon—
when it wanes, when it is on the way out—
he whispers to the derelicts who come to urinate

and the bums hear with muffled ears and translate
"Paris of the West" into a John Wayne film
they lurch down the streets proclaiming God
has resurrected the Duke and brought him to Detroit
the statue whispers to the moon
you are my brother, paradise lost

five dollars a day rushes gold into the street
much like the sun
the sun which shines and then goes away
and nothing less is thought of it
it is the movement of time
the sun,
the moon,
the next day comes

1967

And so I have been longer with you than anyone.
Taking you into me.
We become each other.
I was born in your fire.
Your smoke is in my lungs.

Teresa Tan

I will never understand the city

Inspired by a walk in Greektown

sometimes I listen for the ocean's whisper
in old coke bottles
pale green as aquamarine
or crouching by an overpass at night, watch
for spirits lurking in bone bridges.

I found yellow herringbones beached
and flayed on every parking lot,
and from here the lights are insect swarms
in the industrial thicket.
but I can't hear the angels from downtown.

stones and bones and ancient rhythm
higher wisdom beneath my feet
tear it out and pave it over
no compassion in concrete.

lose me in this place,
to this throbbing machine
and look for me here.
I'll be splintered

or shot with sunlight
or burnishing an old spoon.

shimmer like rings on a gasoline rainbow
or the ash scattered by your cigarette.

meanwhile
every street lamp singing
in its socket
pays tribute to a star.

Keith Taylor

Detroit Dancing 1948

in memoriam: Leo Golus

Everyone home from the war with stories
to tell. Except me, of course. Just a bit
too young to know the horrors of Iwo,
Normandy, the Bulge, I spent the duration
peddling popcorn outside a theater on
Gratiot; later, groceries at the Market.
No woman would be wowed by any yarn
I could spin. And I'd never win a turkey
with my looks. You see, everyone needs
an angle. At the Polish National Alliance
in Hamtramck, the women gathered dutifully
around their returning heroes, wide-eyed
in the presence of such courage. But when
they danced, they danced alone, their arms
circling the smoke from a hundred cigarettes.
With luck one might find another woman
anxious to show her grace. Think of it,
years spent watching two women, nineteen
or twenty, sway each other over
the stained floor. So I taught myself dancing,
downstairs, at home, in the old neighborhood,
humming "Moonlight Serenade" for rhythm,
waltzing the broom, my partner, from coal bin
to canning jars, learning to finish

with a flourish (dipping its bristled head
gently toward the cement), until I could
walk into any club anywhere in the city,
pick out any woman, turn her once
across the floor, and, if I didn't sweep
her off her feet, I'd hear at least
(and this was almost enough, then)
that I was certainly light on mine.

Dennis Teichman

Uprising

"We'll begin by killing all the subversives, then their (collaborators
then their sympathizers, then the indifferent, and finally the timid.
Argentine Gen. Iberico St. Jean, Dec. 1976

All the racism that built the factories shot its flames
into the Sunday sky. The house as bullet the city as heart.
The world once again gets its industrial passion play.

" . . . Ladies and Gentlemen, on behalf of the City of Detroit
and FORDODGM Conglomerate I would like to welcome you
to this year's major struggle . . . as we move along you'll notice
on your left there's nothing left . . . merely charred individual
nightmares reenacting the bitter memories of such notable
incidents as the torment of Dr. Ossian Sweet and the Belle Isle
riots of the 40s . . . and if you'll just shift your attention
to the right you'll find the hi-res screens
portraying meeting after meeting between responsible
community groups such as Gov. Romney, The Irish Mayors Club
Suburban Factor, Inc., and the Loyal Sons of the Laughing CEO's . . .
please make sure that you move along the paths demanded,
you may smoke if you'd like and any memories you have
we will gladly confuse, distort, and autograph at your convenience . . . "

All the talk in the foundries and kitchens trying to explain to someone
anyone no one that there comes a time when your hands

can finally match the hurt in your heart. The house the voice the city the
  prod.

" . . . They drag my daddy out the bar, beat im, told him no shit
come in here. This after 14 hours at the Bessemer, and he was
so thirsty he need a damn drink, that's all . . . Please be seated
take a number I'm sorry we can't help your kind
if you don't want to help yourself . . . All the time I'm in this
big house starin' at white babies, white babies, wondering
what my own kids be doing . . . They may work here, but they'll
never fuckin' live here. This is Dearborn, buster, not some
backwater goddam southern town . . . We got pride, we got
anger, little else. Houses gone, stores gone; double nothin' . . .
Well, I got me a big 'ol shotgun and Russ here,
well, he's got one too. Y'all oughta know we can do this
and settle it once for all. Hey, maybe we can git some of
them dumb polacks and jewheads too, that right, Russ? . . .
You have taken our rights of justice and equality, our very lives
as citizens, as human beings and have thrown us
into this burning street. This flaming cauldron is our America;
these children you see here today will remember . . . "

All set for future development, but, to tell you the truth,
that is, if memory serves us correctly, nothing could have
happened here. The videos are brittle with age, acid paper
has shot the words into dust. Contacts with survivors is rare
or unsought. Somehow, we have this problem of violent kids.
Go figure. The house as child, the city itself.

" . . . Hello. You have reached HISTREX. We have the finest
selection of RAH (radically accessorized histories) and OOPS
(operational occluding precedent sequencing) systems
available for your use. If you want our basic menu, please
dial one. If you want CHP's (comprehensive historical pre-texts)
dial two. If you want RAT's (racial augmentation theories)

dial three. Pressing four will
bring you back to the selection menu. Thank you for calling
HISTREX, where History can be what *You* make of it . . ."

Epilogue

Wide angle zigzag around rut and animal into the "encampment,"
St. Aubin/Ferry cross, metro big time bass note to the Heavens,
12 churches, 1 bar, once more now the looming of the next Amerikan
suicide pact plant rising square rigged a track away from meat storage:
"Welcome to Incineratortown," where all's well if its dead
it smells and if its alive it stinks.

Stop in to pay respects, coffee at the chow truck with some guards
and late-leaving electricians . . . "so this is it, this is the political Whoppe
laying on the roadside . . ." no answer, looks with distrust
among the spread of sludge ruts towards the packing houses, . . .
"you think people still see this thing working?" "hell, man,
they're workin' overtime," closer to complaint, closer to mornings
of rotten trash and dirty lingo.

A webbed idea, trap our indifference then segue into gee-whiz when
all that money can buy mixes cheese whip with hog shit and filters
down on your roses, so many miscues to become roadside manor,
like burning plastic or tarp or when the first hoffaesque baggie containing
    wino
stuffed with bottles up avec sterno garni catches in the continual
flame; no sense to plot your path by watching which way the 4 x 4's
brown tire it out of sight, this air goes where you go
and that's what this sad haze meant.

Stephen Tudor

Factories along the River

The "thereness" of you—seen from
a distance—that pleasing, happy,
foolish, aesthetic, philosophical
perspective of you that we can adopt
as long as we're not employees.

I mean you, Mister Detroit Edison
on the River St. Clair. And you,
Wyandotte Chemical, downriver from
Motor City, though you are now
torn down. And you, Medusa Cement.

That is to say, you have the
blank, monumental air of cathedrals,
museums, opera houses, state
capitals, though you're merely
a steel works or power plant.

I cite Uniroyal Tire, that was
west of the Belle Isle Bridge. *Ubi
sunt?* And the elegant Imperial Oil
Limited, at Sarnia with its Gothic
cracking towers and perpetual flame.

Perhaps it's that motoring upstream
it takes us so long to pass you by.

We're often drawn in towards you by
wind or current or by the strategy of
cutting corners where the river bends.

Think of words we associate with you:
industry, enterprise, manufacture; yet
you transcend language—we ourselves, it
is, with all our stepping back, who fall to
"weather," "fatigue," "hunger," "loss of self."

You're the stuff of sidings, tramways,
welded or riveted steel, slag ablaze,
mounted cranes, blow offs, conveyors
patiently edging coal, limestone, salt,
sand, taconite into conical tips.

To you, bulk cargo vessels—ore and
aggregate carriers, tankers, barges,
scrappers, grain boats, traders in
gypsum—are creatures of use, so many
watertight sleds, carts, hand trucks.

In our greed for words we take to
ourselves what we mistake for your
speech. We will not learn our own,
though the light on the river changes,
and you recede even as we approach.

Detroit River North to South

You are lacing your boots at the Windmill
Point Light and Lakeside Trailer Court where
the river slides out of Lake St. Clair.

You are mixing Manhattans at Peche Island
over on the Canadian side. An owl in
the last tree in Ontario winks once.

You are saving string on Belle Isle.
Your hair is perfect. You have tap danced
across the water from Hiram Walker's.

You are honing hatchets at Medusa Cement.
One look and they head for the hills. You
are a singer of sexy songs in downtown Windsor.

You are hoeing tomatoes at the Ren Cen and
Cobo Hall. Listen to someone who is sincere
and likewise wants to ravish you, today.

You are kissing boyfriends at the door of
the USPO. This is next to the Port of
Detroit, where you're tucking in your blouse.

You are ironing shirts in the middle of the
Ambassador Bridge. What's the difference?
It's Saturday, and traffic's backed up as it is.

You are loosening your belt at Northwest
Steamship, South Windsor. Meanwhile there are gulls
fishing in small boats and apricots in the sky.

You are scratching your sheepdog's ears
at Great Lakes Steel Division, National
Steel Corporation, pride of Zug Island.

You are changing film at Ontario Hydro and
have a room to paint in the chaste boutique of
Wyandotte Chemical, opposite Fighting Island.

You are pruning the rose of the fourth asteroid in
a blue tearoom on Grosse Ile. Brass violins serenade
Amherstburg and the Livingstone Channel.

You are pretending to listen to the deacon of
mallards at Detroit River Light in Lake Erie.
No one has free will. You are the seasons.

Chris Tysh

6/To Rehearse

d the bastard child of the engineer

d not to be confused with *dépense*

d must have trembled all the way

d would thus hang on the fact

d index of endurance

d lacunary

d ill state, a transfer of

d detached from

d in the event of desire

d shell of a city

d keys its inhabitants to disperse

d tardy frame at no charge

d penned in flimsy letters

d grief

d bereaved, watches over

d early arrival in very small numbers

d sparse columns, the gendered aspect of evening

d ordinance, the same finality

d forces things apart

7/As Quoted Before

the river had always been there
before Rouge, Drum, the Locals
and foreigners banging at the gate

I've written this all wrong: d, the raft,
sailcloth introduce a marine presence
anchoring the weight attached to this
pantomime. One would thus witness the self
as other, a prison guard making his rounds
or perhaps a back alley of safes, a mute
scene where kitchen knives are used instead
of soft-metaled gears, painted green, later
black with red striping. On the abominable
roads and ribbon farms Model T destiny
refers the audience to ornery car men.
CRANK & ROLL 'EM out of any shit hole.
CRACK sex shots switch from $5 day
to the sullen presence of WORKERS!
& COMRADES! Women would drop their panties,
get married, no need to include them Ford
prophesied. Such is the curse of d: nipples
mirrored in contempt, her nameless body
inseparable from mating with the compulsive
machinery. A short stiff brush there in
the dark while duck, muskrat and men run
down for protection. Say construction,
say giant steel girders like passive impotent
birdcage manufacturers take hold of the
erotic metaphor to cast her down, alack,
under the shooting stars of this new language.

George Tysh

Aire

Supposing a globe of black wavers as the room breathes

cylinders of attention which rise—our guests also rise

in their travels on hands powered by unknown balloons.

Unloading crates of vocal water, the tom-tom elevators in

the background lift. Supposing a neckline in touch with

an element of desire penetrates the cloud on a postage

stamp. Rain on the scene hissing slowly could breathe

in hallways. Floor above floor, room to room, the geyser

pours out a voice in childlike doses of continuity: "your

shoes, your lips, your waist," etc.

●◆●

Babes

There are pinholes in the social fabric through which we see

their glass figurines. White hearts, white as living with slow

access to boundless green, who remember countries hardly there.

A somnambulist interferes at the summit of white around us, the

spinning halos and whirling rings of the act. Like a four-sided

corner in the brain, prodded by spikes, dabbed by thighs. We

turn up the treble and tune in plexiglas wafers of celestial lunch,

pink asteroids that click in diamond heels. The voice that wakes

is them in high C, piercing the stillness in nylons, unfolding

a couch of hand-held dreams, the hide-a-bed of night where we wait.

Melanie Van der Tuin

Detroit

I tried fiercely
not to set down roots,
tried to imagine Detroit
as one of those windy, slush-spattered
bus stops
along Woodward,
a stop between decisions

I moved back home

But I was one of those
tumbleweed plastic Farmer Jack's bags
that billows across the Lodge
then floats on,
an air-filled urban ghost

I wouldn't stay long

I would be smiling Farmer Jack
stamped in red on soft, tan plastic,
brushing across commuters' windshields,
never closer to anyone's countertop
than a load of groceries

But nobody warned me

Nobody warned me
that I would *like* the sleepy
hum of campus
late at night

Nobody warned me
that old brick
would start to feel more comfortable than carpeting,
that people inside Johnny's would be
talking about films and
transistors
and break-ups

Nobody warned me
the waitress would start to call me *honey*

I tried,
when I felt it starting to happen,
I tried to tell myself
that these were trivial
small comforts

I forgot
that small comforts
are everything

On the way home,
wildflowers would
squeeze out from between
highway divider blocks

The Ambassador Bridge
and the Fisher
burned

gold teeth
into the night sky

And the old train station
kept watch
with dark
hollowed-out eyes

Nobody told me
that silent men fish by the river at night
to the endless slosh
and waving stars
and headlights,
that the diesel mail trucks
churn all night long
through the huge post office
on Fort

The sounds became familiar words:
highway-purr-through-classroom-window
ancient-pipes-at-war-at-midnight
dog-on-concrete-kicking-glass

Some days
when I wasn't watching
my feet began to set tiny roots
into certain wooden floors
and my voice inherited a creak

Once, I found a yellowed
air raid drill sign
hanging in a classroom in State Hall,
the building crouched around it
still intact
some fifty years later

While fifteen minutes away
orchids bloomed in the Belle Isle Conservatory,
and palm trees,
holly, bananas

Winter on the island
covered the frost with ice white sheets
pierced by deer tracks
and crisscrossed by slender skis

Nobody told me about
the peacefulness of the moon through the reeds there,
or the history
dripping from the eaves
of decaying Victorian houses
downtown.
The spirits along Trumbull
listen to old blues
and on overcast days
you can see them sitting on porches,
waiting for the rain

I never saw them before,
never ventured far from the old, red trolleys
we rode as children

Now, sometimes,
I watch the Greyhound buses
pull into the station on Howard,
passengers' faces framed by an eerie
green light,
staring out at their first shadows of Detroit

To them,
I am part of the landscape,

part of an old city
struggling to be remembered

Bottles sparkle in the snow below them,
and plastic bags flap in bare trees
like old, weathered birds

My roots have taken here
outstretched like the maze of branches underground
that makes the concrete buckle

Mandela Comes to Motown

We had stopped singing
our voices drowned
beneath the pained bridge of despair

We had settled for synthesized blues
and unrebellious saxophones
Even slave songs lost refrain

We had stopped singing
until you came
and we saw that you still dance

Chant on US-80

for Tony Liuzzo

Tony hears the
Hears the footsteps
Of his mama
Of his mama

Walking softly
Walking softly

Down the highway
Down the highway

He can see her
He can see her
Moving onward
Moving onward
To the place where
To the place where
Freedom hides
Where freedom hides

Do you hear the
Hear the footsteps
Of his mama
Of his mama
As you make your
As you make your
Way to freedom
Way to freedom

You must listen
You must listen
For her footsteps
For her footsteps

As she leads her
As she leads her
Silent army
Silent army
On to justice
On to justice

On to justice

Anca Vlasopolos

March of Dimes, April in Detroit

Some point to this house here and say, This is where
I grew up, or a building with broken windows, or simply
a space, I went to school on this spot; my cousin lives
three blocks over, my mother on the other side of town,
my son manages a drugstore in the next neighborhood.

In the twelve-and-a-half miles we march—it could be
five thousand—I have few things to point out for my daughter.
Look, diving ducks in the crook of the river's arm
cradling Belle Isle, look, a kinglet darting swifter
than thought in the barely leafed crab by a parking structure
deserted today, Sunday, downtown. Look, what has been here
since life took these forms, only less of it now, we know.

As we surge up the old riverfront, Jefferson, past
the second station, stamps and smiles, water, juice, apples,
first aid, it comes into sight, the odd Federal Building,
old stone colonial with a black glass and steel wing slapped on
in the fifties to show we meant business, not aesthetics.

At last, look, I say, the place where they tried to make
a natural American woman of me—interviews, oaths, deep
suspicion for the missing year by the man who'd not thought
it important to read our dossier, then, to me, this man
whose own name is an Italian choir of angels with no
English equivalence,

you must change your name, your first name I mean, so
unAmerican, your last (with a smug wink) you'll change
in the course of time.

Late Encounter

Eastern Market is packing up as afternoon
clamps on its tight damp lid. I hear a voice,
ever louder, behind me.
GirlFRIEND! GirlFRIEND!
More and more urgent, and the cloppity clops
of an approach from which I hasten away
through the cavernous hangar.
A feather tap on my shoulder.
And here he stands like an apparition, rather he hunches
in others' clothes, on his crutches.
"I don't go by the college no more. 'Cause they
keep busting me," he answers my unasking.
"Got something to help me out?"
A dollar bill flutters from hand to outstretched hand.
Then, again, this man of an age with me, born
a month earlier almost to the day,
who every mid-September wanted something
a little extra 'cause it was his birthday, says
into my silence,
"I just lost my mother."

Tyrone, I confess, here where you can't hear me,
the shock of meeting you in this semidark, my fearful mirror,
    finding that you had had a mother you just lost,
    you who, cut adrift from all nets but your own
    like me plucked out of context
    looking as if you'd sprung up

just as you appear, no compensation for the pang
of birth,
as if there never was a youthful mother,
      honey of generation . . .
Tyrone, blot on my conscience, mon semblable,
my double

Ron Allen's Poem

the chef in the kitchen
cooks your heart
serves it to you
on a platter of your choosing;

only the spice is his.
what meat you do not like
is yours and yours alone;

and if the heart is cleft in two,
don't blame him, for the heart belongs to you.

Literally, for Elegance You Went

for George Tysh

1.

And when "those in the know" thought
        you wouldn't have it in you to go,
you went the distance—sure-footed across a decade of
pimpsuits who thought they ran you
        and corny mutherfuckers
talking much shit

while you simply, and literally, for elegance
put your money your heart your body
where your mouth was;
        roamed that funky urban landscape,
rode out along that suburban loneliness
to meet with moneymen on our behalf, George, to
bring back fire to the empty lots, the abandoned
urban rust pots sad ass city, Dee-Straught,
city drunk on Taylorism
        hating itself, which you embraced to forage
      what others would not even see,
    and toiled and planted,
and tilled and planted.

2.

        Literally, for elegance, you went alone down
      hallways of corporate art studio academe
    junkyard factory town boardroom bargain matinee
to buy back our flesh.
    to strike a deal with the devil and make that elegance grow;
      you had to cross that lonesome valley,
        you had to cross it by yourself, you and Chris.

3.

And when all we thought we ever could be
was ugliness
      you said no, no, there will be elegance here.
and so you went alone, just Chris and you,
son of Hamtramck, radical,
sociopolitical, artworker, you,
      said, no, no, there will be elegance here,

and so you went on your own damn dime
while others hid in their indifference,
planted the very seeds we neglected, wept and prayed
before the face of Mammon when he said
"you'll owe me for this"
put your soul on the table and played draw poker
with the devil, for us,
and we loved you for it,
though we never thanked you, that you
tended the fields out back of the art institute boardroom,
tended the fields out back of the artless council boredom,
corporate art studio academe
junkyard factory town bargain matinee
to make that elegance grow,
to make that elegance grow

David Watson

Trust Jesus

for Susan Kramer

"*At least one crucified at every corner.*"
Charles Simic

A painter who cuts hair to buy supplies,
talking my ears off while trimming around them,
told me, "I was feeling bleak,
went to swim it out of me at the Downtown Y.
It was one of those interminably gray
Detroit February days, all the houses caved in
and the beggars walking on stumps.
And I saw sprayed on a mailbox, *Trust Jesus.*
It's written all over town by the same lonely fool.
Trust Jesus, I said to myself. This is Detroit.
The '90s. You've gotta give me more than that."

Barrett Watten

Tibet

    (low yellow Renaissance towers
    frame Ocean Beach
    mood of Cerulean blue
    or copper overlaid with blue plate

Sympathetic to the sweet cypresses
a whale rises from the blue fumes forming a cloud—
the mayors of the respective towns are out parading.

A crowd gathers, passing the bottle around
some standing in a long curving line.

    Some are talking
    the waves, etc.
    the bigger the better—

The troops are departing by boat
I can see them
    but think of myself—
    as better than nature.

There is nothing of the Cliff House worth noting.
The polypus behind me feels like a cancer—
sinews connecting Detroit and Sacramento
muscles of the Corn Belt and Valley.

The odd sun shines elsewhere
on a world of republics
the men and women who built them
as any sickness of the remote.

Each penetration of the earth by the sun
is a point on the map
solved by four colors
in the mind's eye a virgin Iris and her way.

But I, enstatic
a clean plain
at endless altitude
inside the color brown

am formally known as Tibet—
the indifference.

FOOTNOTE TO TIBET

Tibet is thinking
China is nature

China is the Manifest
Dream of Tibet

Now China is the Air Force
and Tibet is the air for flight

Now China is the air
and Tibet is the ether

Now China is the ether
and Tibet is the air—

What about this
suppression of Tibet?

from *Under Erasure*

> *The assembly line advances,*
> > *to add*
> *Each new station to your machine . . .*

> *An increment of time that wants*
> *Everything to stop,*
> > *I break apart . . .*

> *In a democratic art,*
> > *to represent*
> *Rouge River in photographs, 1947 . . .*

The city of Detroit under weather times a variable
On this day of the revolutionary calendar in 1789
Its blue bunting on tables keeps percipients away . . .

While partners sleep in the night of their desires
As options opening up advantages for future trade
She reinvests in later under our protective gaze . . .

> *A careful reproduction of parts*
> *In any language,*
> > *if already known . . .*

These are everyday matters I write about every day
Even as robots attacked mutants in Heavenly Peace
A refreshment gave us pause during *Giants vs. Reds . . .*

BARRETT WATTEN   381

Is always to be learned,
                    clouds
That communicate with each other . . .

A thought exterior to yourselves
In training flights,
                    thundering jets . . .

A better paperback to read than anyone could write
Or simply that he is more aware of things being now
Like they were then than it will ever become again . . .

In quotation marks,
                    if understood
As not preceding understanding . . .

That to facilitate relations with others I want
To give a perfect theory of knowledge as incomplete
And the view of the city below will be first-rate . . .

. . . .

Whose one possible emotion is an admission of loss
Ranging from joy to grief in its plotted accidents
Reduced to atoms you project as if to covering song . . .

Until only she controls fantasy
Of a use,
                    and I watch the news . . .

A lattice of commutes,
                    whose routes
Arrayed in color-coded dispatches . . .

Mark his identity as an exchange

At the hub of information.
                        "1989" . . .

Its machines answering back but only one move ahead
As rats push their buttons for continuous soft hits
Other format configurations are no longer accepted . . .

You press fast forward and remain seated in place
If a touchstone is xeroxed many times in succession
As among islands we hop only from pleasure to pain . . .

                The industry,
                        a component designed
                To produce cars at the same rate . . .

                As destinations with exit signs
                I invariably select,
                                to demonstrate . . .

Tiny windows at a distance turn surfaces to plane
She is the victim of abstract explanations in depth
Of original ideas rewritten to applicable technique . . .

But you plan to be incorporated by the work of each
In a high-density display that allows all to select
Any of 58,000 shapes resolved into individual lines . . .

                What words can mean,
                                if each frame
                Of its blank as a vanishing point . . .

                Approximates self-consciousness
                In clouds,
                        our pseudo-objectivity . . .

Wants elsewhere to be,
                    I will go
And be happy with their results . . .

Kim Webb

Human Nature

The Polish woman in ten yards of floral print
Arcane laughter episodic
A laugh common when dreading the thunder of storms
A laughing horde of angry waitresses
Theoretical labor automatically mobile
An argument of nature—spilled words
Technological conversation congealed as nouns
Granted knives welding an operations manual
I speak from the rectory of the unconscious
Rose gardens, quiet desks / robes to conceal their affections
All forces lose steam approaching me . . . the rains gentle
I speak into a storm once a week it is all scripted out
Meals arrive salted, one waitress invariably takes sides
Drop the god damn knife
Into a Euro concern for space
Dense as a Jewish cemetery heavy and practical like a tortoise shell
The eyes of the convenience store clerk wild for an instant
They bounce off gun metal before falling nondescript litter
A city's promises break the sidewalks winter by winter
The fast and slow of it
The scale, the profanity tacked to what remains of profundit wood
The weight that taxes each deep breath
I make it all lose steam
I am a woman in rubber gloves cleaning my screen door
Bright yellow gloves and hot soapy water

Mary Ann Wehler

They Walked a Mile for a Camel, the Man's Cigarette

His fingernails drummed on the white enamel table.
My father sat in the kitchen. He pulled a pack of Camels
from his shirt pocket, then tapped the box. He stared
at the vacant wall. I can still see the two nicotine stained
fingers, the long hard nails. He was proud of their strength,
so tough, he had special clippers.

Dying from lung cancer in the upstairs flat was Joe Bielman.
Every day when my father came home from General Motors,
he went up to visit. He hollered up the hall stairs,
Joe, how the hell are you? How's the world treatin' you?
They argued politics, told a few jokes. Soon,
Mr. Bielman would start coughing from laughter.

I listened from the hallway, had never known anyone
with cancer. When my father came down, he sat in
the kitchen, tapped his fingernails on the table, handled
that pack of Camels, stared at the wall. In January,
Mr. Bielman stopped getting out of bed. My father
went up to visit but it was quiet now. He didn't stay
long, came down and sat tapping his fingernails.

I don't remember the funeral. My father carried that same
pack of Camels in his pocket for a year. He bought
a new Chevrolet. No one was allowed to smoke in it.
Gum was in the ash tray.

Karen Williams

Tearing Down "N" Building at Old Eloise Hospital for a New Golf Course

He was sunken, black,
filled with the miseries as he watched "N" building
crumble into tomorrow's dust,
beam by beam,
floor by floor,
window by window,
brick by brick.

They warned him not to go there,
where the stench of ancient urine
rose from porcelain shrouds.
Maybe it was his own,
when highly excited, he never could
hold his water.

Cane in one hand,
fractured brick in the other,
he motioned for his son to walk him closer.
"Uh Uh," he instructed, closer.
"This is where your mother and I first held you brother and sister,"
he remembered for long dead twins born in hallowed sterile halls.

"And this is where they cared,"
he pointed upwards at shattered windows,
"for coal dust, alcohol, chil'ren with polio."

My night job here was my first after the war.
Folks back then wasn't too keen
on niggers mopping and hauling shit in the daytime."

The wreckers coughed more bitter dust
as guts of his truth heaped on sweat-dampened fields
to be removed before new monuments of condos and golf tees
would soon stand tall like forbidden to him tumblers of gin,
a young man's erections.

The old man squeezed harder the brick,
its fine, cruel particles imprinting his creasing parts
as tomorrow's dust from the home of his tension mounted
and neighborhood golfers sharpened their swing.

Tyrone Williams

The Grace of God

I walked in late for work
and found a note in lieu of bark,
teeth and finger: "level the shelves."

I was pulling cans and boxes to attention

when I came face to face with the "o"
of a long barrel, black as the mask
that wrinkled thrice: "Let's go, bro'."

The aisle went on forever . . .

A year later—or the year before?—
jackknifed in the front seat—
"Let's kill these motherfuckers."

When they dumped us out on our feet, we kept
running, we didn't look back, we did
as we were told.

Years later, a few years back, a plane
landed too late, coinciding
with the yank on a mask, the pull on a plug . . .

What happened?

We did as we were told
to do, we kept running, we didn't look back,

until we thought we were out of range

and we slowed to a walk
and I dropped to my knees
where the aisle stopped.

Alternative Difference

As always I was on my own,
waiting for a woman I had known
once, the shape of all my fallen stars:
a bowl of chips, waiting to be dipped
in salsa, waiting to be washed away
in a guzzle of Dos Equis, in a Spanish rendition
of "I Say A Little Prayer," mesmerized
by ersatz Aztec masks, nodding
at the bar and dreaming of Brazil
at Main and Third in Royal Oak,
of a drunken Robin at the Gotham Cafe,
warbling along with Cole Porter
spinning in the deco jukebox.
When I came to in Union Street—
or was it Verne's? Maybe the Bronx,
or maybe it was even Z's . . .
I don't know, all I know
is that I tried to walk out
to get some air, but the world,
masquerading as a door of glass,
met me head on, and when I lost,

I left a shock of white foundation
and oil from oily black hair on the pane.
I staggered in retreat, stunned,
dressed in all black, obviously blonde.

Many Marvelously Colored Memories

*Dedicated to the Marvelettes and all the
other forgotten girl groups*

SOULFUL SULTRY HUNTRESSES
SHOOTING SHARP LYRICS LASSOES
AS THEY CAPTURE OUR HEARTS
BY OUR EARS
MAKING EVEN WAITING FOR A LETTER
A NOBLE BUT TRAGIC PREOCCUPATION

LOST AMIDST THE MANY MAGICAL
MUSICAL MOMENTS OF MOTOWN
STANDING IN THE SHADOW OF OUR LOVE
AND OF MAN MADE LESSER STARS

GRANDE JEUNE FILLES
ABOVE A "MERE GIRLS GROUP"
SUPERIOR TO THE SUPREMES
AND MUCH MORE VIBRANT THAN
MARTHA R AND THE V'S

THE LEADER'S DEEP RICH URBAN VOICE
DID NOT CROSS OVER WELL
DID NOT RISE AS HIGH AS SMOKE
NOR AS DIAPHANOUS AS PSEUDO-DIVA DIANA

LOST EVEN TO THE LOST 45 STATIONS

THESE FOUR MARVELOUS VOICES
COMING OUT OF INKSTER
AS STRONG AS WCHB'S RADIO SIGNALS
WITH THEIR MAGIC TOUCH
REACHING OUT TO BE CAPTURED
BY LOVERS CAPTURED BY THEIR SONGS

Where Did Her Love Go?

       for Florence Ballard

       Flo don't know

This Girl Dreamed
dreamed dreams on vinyl
to the 45th degree in platinum and gold
primed by songs from basement rehearsals
to blue light dreams

She lost the lead only
to eventually lose her grip
beehived and lamed
a star divided by the power of three
and then reduced by one
will implode with its brilliance
being its own instrument of destruction

Her death was foretold
by the oracles of the blues
and confirmed by Voyagers'
view of Saturn's rings
like the lost wax process
her essence was extracted

leaving only a fragile shell
a thing of beauty for others
to collect, to consume.

Aretha is an exception
maybe it's because she is afraid to fly.

ALVIN AUBERT
52 "You'd Have to See It"
This poem refers to the controversial sculpture designed by Robert Graham as a tribute to Detroit's world heavyweight boxing champion, Joe "brown bomber" Louis. It is located in downtown Detroit across from Hart Plaza.

FARUQ Z. BEY
57 "Kantos"
Tyree Guyton: Detroit artist who created the internationally acclaimed neighborhood art project entitled The Heidelberg Project on Detroit's near eastside (see Hildreth's "The Heidelberg Project").

DONNA BROOK
76 "People Don't Die Just So You Can Write a Poem about Them"
This poem refers to the 1980 suicide death of Bradley Jones, a well-known Wayne State University/Cass Corridor artist from the 1960s, who was friends with this poet and Ken Mikolowski (referred to as Ken in the poem).

MARY ANN CAMERON
82 "Haiku '84"
'84: Refers to the year the Detroit Tigers won the World Series in a spectacular season.

LEON CHAMBERLAIN
84 "Highland Park"
Highland Park is not only a neighborhood, but also the site where Henry Ford built his first assembly plant, which was designed by well-known Detroit architect Albert Kahn.

ESPERANZA M. CINTRON
89 "Street Market Requiem"
"unfortunate vessels": Booker T. Washington, "Atlanta Compromise."
"the best street sweepers": Martin Luther King, Jr., speech; opening for (Detroit D.J.) Mojo's show.
Macon Deads and Luther Nedeeds: reference to sisters Morrison (*Song of Solomon*) and Naylor (*Linden Hills*) respectively.

TOI DERRICOTTE
112 "Blackbottom"
Blackbottom: Legendary African American neighborhood of the early 20th century near downtown Detroit.

MARK DONOVAN
113 "HIP 1"
HIP: Stands for Horizons In Poetry Series, the longest running urban poetry series in Detroit.
Cass Corridor: Neighborhood near Wayne State's campus known for its lively street life and its crime.

JOAN GARTLAND
126 "Egyptian Gallery in August: Detroit 1994"
Egyptian Gallery: Refers to the nationally acclaimed Detroit Institute of Arts' Egyptian art exhibit in 1994.

MICHELE GIBBS
134 "Message from the Meridian"
Paradise Valley: Thriving African American business and entertainment district during the first half of the twentieth century, located near Black Bottom on Detroit's near east side.
Black Bottom: (see Derricotte's "Blackbottom")

AURORA HARRIS

147 "Jitterbug, Jazz and the Graystone"

Paradise Valley: (see Gibbs' "Message from the Meridian")

Black Bottom: (see Derricotte's "Blackbottom")

References to artifacts and facts are from the *History of The Graystone* as provided by the Graystone Jazz Museum; lines 23, 25, 26, 38, and 39 are from Mr. Jenkins' account of his life as told in *Untold Tales, Unsung Heroes, An Oral History of Detroit's African American Community, 1918–1967* by Elaine Latzman Moon: Detroit Urban League Inc., Wayne State University Press, 1994; lines 52–62 are from a combination of Cuba Austin's account of his involvement on the jazz circuit, and other famous jazz musicians' first hand accounts of the history of jazz from *The Story of Jazz as Told By the Men Who Made It: HEAR ME TALKIN' TO YA* by Nat Shapiro and Nat Hentoff, Dover Press, New York, reprinted 1966. The original book was published by Rinehart and Company, Inc., 1955.

Thanks to Board Member Ella for the opportunity to write this piece, Beans Bowles for Mr. Jenkins' nickname (Jitterbug) and the places he frequented (Brown's Bar, Freddy Guinyard's), Mr. Lahab, Shawna Kitt, Mrs. Dozier, and the rest of the Graystone Jazz Museum Board Members for their love, kindness, support, and a home for The World Voice Poetry Series.

BILL HARRIS

152 "Elegy"

Blackbottom: (see Derricotte's "Blackbottom")

Paradise: Refers to Paradise Valley (see Gibbs' "Message from the Meridian").

ROBERT HAYDEN

155 "Elegies for Paradise Valley"

Paradise Valley: (see Gibbs' "Message from the Meridian")

ERROL A. HENDERSON

161 "Support Your Local Police: What We Pay Our Police For?"

This poem refers to the historical tension between Detroit citizens and the Detroit Police. Malice Green, Gary Glenn, Boyd, and Bethune, names that are well-known in Detroit, are Detroiters who have died as a result of police brutality and excess force. STRESS (Stop The Robberies, Enjoy Safe Streets) was a Detroit police undercover operation that targeted African American males through covert tactics that entrapped Detroit citizens.

JERRY HERRON

169 "The Passion of Edsel Ford"

This poem, told through the eyes of Edsel Ford, son of Henry Ford, mentions many names associated with his father's business. Harry Bennett was a despised anti-union employee, and Walter Reuther was the founding president of the UAW. Dr. William Valentiner, a German, became director of the Detroit Institute of Arts in 1921 and was a close friend to Edsel Ford. Diego Rivera, the Mexican artist, came to Detroit in 1932, with his wife, Frida Kahlo, to paint a series of murals at the Detroit Institute of Arts. Ernest Kanzler was Edsel Ford's brother-in-law. Kanzler, an attorney, was married to the elder sister of Edsel's wife. Fair Lane was the home of Henry Ford in Dearborn and St. Clair refers to Edsel's home on Lake St. Clair in Grosse Pointe. Biographical information is borrowed (and elaborated) from, Robert Lacey, *Ford: The Men and the Machine* (Boston: Little, Brown and Co., 1986).

ELLEN HILDRETH

175 "The Heidelberg Project"

Heidelberg Project: The controversial, internationally acclaimed, block-long work of art founded by artist Tyree Guyton, his grandfather Sam Mackey, and former wife Karen Guyton in 1986 on Detroit's east side and sustained for more than a decade, despite partial demolitions in 1991 and 1999 by the city of Detroit. The decaying neighborhood of the Heidelberg Project was transformed, with the assistance of neighbors and fellow artists who helped festoon its houses, trees, sidewalks, and so on with paint and salvaged objects such as shoes, dolls, suitcases, hubcaps, and other urban detritus. See also Bey's "Kantos."

OLIVER LAGRONE

207 "I Heard the Byrd"

This poem refers to Donald Byrd, a famous trumpeter from Detroit who holds a Ph.D. in ethnomusicology.

M. L. LIEBLER

224 "Save the Frescoes That Are Us"

Rivera Murals: Diego Rivera was commissioned by the Ford family to paint major murals on the walls of the Detroit Institute of Arts in the early 1930s.

Rivera's Lenin Headed Mural: Refers to Rivera's Rockefeller Center murals painted after Detroit's, but painted over because Rivera included a painting of V.I. Lenin's head.

NAOMI LONG MADGETT

229 "Good News"

Clad dimes and quarters: Coins originally made of silver and now composed of copper sandwiched between a cover of cupro-nickel, another metal base.

RAYMOND P. MCKINNEY

238 "Things Ain't What They Used to Be"

valley paradise: Refers to Paradise Valley (see Gibbs' "Message from the Meridian")

Black bottom: (see Derricotte's "Blackbottom")

JESSICA CARE MOORE

257 "Black Coals with Diamond Hearts"

Bad Boys: Nickname for Detroit Pistons' back-to-back championship team.

JAN MORDENSKI

261 "Like Colavito"

The 1960 season saw changes in the Detroit club when the young hard-hitting Rocky Colavito was traded for the seasoned Harvey Kuenn. Ironically, "The Rock," who played right field in the 60s, was no longer in the line-up when the Tigers won the pennant eight years later. On January 1, 1961, Briggs Stadium's name was officially changed to Tiger Stadium.

EUGENE B. REDMOND

301 "Aerolingual Poet of Prey"

This poem, dedicated to Alvin Aubert, mentions his books *South Louisiana, Against the Blues, Feeling Through* and his journal, *Obsidian,* which he brought to Detroit in the late 1970s.

LESLIE REESE
306 "I Love You (The Heidelberg Project)"
Heidelberg Project: (see Bey's "Kantos" and Hildreth's "The Heidelberg Project")

TRINIDAD SÁNCHEZ, JR.
323 "Let Us Stop This Madness"
S.O.S.A.D.: Save Our Sons And Daughters, a Detroit-based organization formed by mothers of murdered Detroit children to stop the violence.

STEVEN SCHREINER
326 "Passion Fruit"
Vernor's plant: The main bottling plant for Detroit's unique version of ginger ale soda was produced near the WSU campus.

RENÉE TAMBEAU
348 "Renaissance"
Detroit is the first industrial city to have died. In the 1970s the Renaissance Center was built on the waterfront in downtown Detroit. Detroit, with its efforts to revitalize itself, became known as the Renaissance City.

salt: In ancient times, salt was used as a form of salary. The phrase "worth his salt" comes from this.

"The Paris of the West": Detroit, in its heyday, was called "The Paris of the West."

five dollars a day: In 1914, Henry Ford offered automobile employees the possibility of earning five dollars a day. This drew thousands of people into the city looking for money and opportunity.

349 "1967"
1967 was the year of Detroit's worst race riot. This riot was considered one of the most disastrous in the U.S. during the 1960s. It is also the year the poet was born.

CHRIS TYSH
361 "6/To Rehearse"
d: Refers to the city of Detroit.
362 "7/As Quoted Before"

DRUM: Refers to the Dodge Revolutionary Urban Movement, an African American organization that sprouted up in Detroit factories to counter unfair treatment of minority workers.

d: Refers to the city of Detroit.

HILDA VEST

370 "Chant on US-80"

Viola Liuzzo, a white civil-rights activist of the 1960s and Wayne State student, was gunned down on US-80, a highway that connects Selma and Montgomery, Alabama. In 1982 her son Tony was invited by the Southern Christian Leadership Conference to march along that highway in her memory.

RAYFIELD WALLER

375 "Literally, for Elegance You Went"

This poem refers to the Detroit Institute of Arts because George Tysh, to whom the poem is dedicated, ran a longtime national literary series there in the 1980s.

KAREN WILLIAMS

387 "Tearing Down "N" Building at Old Eloise Hospital for a New Golf Course"

Eloise Hospital: Well-known and much-dreaded mental hospital in the Detroit area.

All the contributors to this volume have lived in the Detroit Metropolitan area at some time during their writing career.

SARAH ADDAE is a longtime Detroit poet who has worked much in the "Cass Corridor" arts scene.

SALADIN AHMED was born in Detroit to parents of Arab and Irish ancestry. His work has appeared in several anthologies, and he is a two-year member of Detroit National Poetry Slam team.

RON ALLEN, well-known Detroit poet and playwright, is a community cultural worker and cofounder of the long-running Horizons In Poetry (H.I.P.) Series in the Cass Corridor. His recent books are *Neon Jawbone Riot* (Weightless Language Press, 2000) and *I Want My Body Back* (Ridgeway Press, 1996).

ALISE ALOUSI is a Detroit poet who first appeared on the Detroit scene in the mid-1980s. She has since gone on to publish many of her poems locally and nationally, including her chapbook *Wearing Doors Away* (Ridgeway Press). She works for Alternatives for Girls, Inc. in Detroit.

MITZI ALVIN, poet and lecturer on topics poetical, is poetry editor for *The Bridge* (a local literary journal with a national reputation), a facilitator for the Adult Learning Center, and a longtime promoter of the Sublime Art in the Detroit and Metropolitan areas. She has one book, *Evidence to the Contrary* (Plainview Press, 1998).

OLIVIA V. AMBROGIO is an undergraduate at Oberlin College. She is the former editor of *Freezer Burn*, and her work has been published in *Red*

Cedar Review, Yemassee, Onionhead, The Herbal Network, and *Controlled Burn.*

ALVIN AUBERT is a two-time National Endowment for the Arts fellowship awardee. His latest collections are *If Winter Come: Collected Poems* (1994) and *Harlem Wrestler* (1995). He is a Wayne State University professor emeritus.

IRVINE BARAT is a retired social science professor. He has published in the U.S. and Canada. Formerly a featured poet on CBC radio program "Crosstown," he is currently a freelance writer. "Four Decades Ago" first appeared in *Running at 60* (self-published chapbook).

FARUQ Z. BEY is a Detroit poet, fiction writer, and award-winning jazz saxophonist. He is the founder of Detroit's legendary sci-fi avant jazz band, Griot Galaxy. Several of his books of poetry and music theory have been published by Ridgeway Press.

SADIQ BEY (formerly known as Sadiq Muhammad) is known as a multi-talented artist. He was the founder of the African World Festival in Detroit and was the founding editor of the *City Arts Review.* He hosted a poetry and jazz program on WDET during the 1970s and 80s. He is currently residing in New York where he performs his work with the group, "The Muse's Boyfriend."

TERRY BLACKHAWK is the author of *Body & Field* from Michigan State University Press and *Trio: Voices from the Myth,* a chapbook from Ridgeway Press. For her work as founder and director of InsideOut, a writers-in-schools program serving Detroit youth, she received a Detroit *Metro Times* Progressive Hero Award and a 2000 Governors' Award in Arts Education from ArtServe Michigan. "February Teacher" first appeared in *Passages North.* "Reader Response" was originally published in *The Comstock Review.*

MELBA JOYCE BOYD is the author of five books of poetry: *Cat Eyes and Dead Wood, Song for Maya, Thirteen Frozen Flamingoes, The Inventory of Black Roses,* and *Letters to Che.* She was an assistant editor at Broadside Press (1972–77). Her poetry has been widely published in journals, anthologized, and translated into German, Italian, and Spanish. She is currently professor and chair of the Department of Africana Studies at Wayne State University. "We Want Our City Back," "The View of Blue," and "The Burial of a Building" were first published in *The Black Scholar.*

JILL WITHERSPOON BOYER is a native Detroiter living in California. She is also the author of *Breaking Camp* (Lotus Press, 1984). "Summers" and "Detroit City" are from *Dream Farmer* (Broadside Press, 1975).

WILLIAM BOYER is a theater director, musician, and author of over a dozen plays, most recently "Marla In-Between," "The Butterfly Flick," and "Birdie on the Back Nine" published by Ridgeway Press (1996).

DONNA BROOK received an M.A.T. from Wayne State's English Department and taught in the Department during the 1970s. She has published four books of poems and, in 1998, a history of the English language for children (*The Journey of English*, Clarion). Both poems are in *A More Human Face*, a collection of her poems published in 1999 by Hanging Loose Press, Brooklyn, NY.

JAMES BURDINE is a graduate of Wayne State University and resides in New York City.

ANTHONY BUTTS is a Wayne State University and Western Michigan University graduate. He is a member of the Carnegie-Mellon University creative writing faculty and the author of *Fifth Season* (New Issues Press, 1997). Both poems in this volume are from that collection.

MARY ANN CAMERON was born in Detroit in 1943. An ex-English teacher, she now reads tarot, interprets dreams, and makes beaded jewelry and hangings.

NORENE CASHEN is a freelance writer and poet. Her poems were first published in *Dispatch*, volume one. She lives in Michigan and contributes frequently to the *Metro Times*.

LEON CHAMBERLAIN is a labor poet. His work has been printed in newspapers, books, anthologies, and magazines. He has read all around the U.S. and on the BBC. He is the author of three books.

HAYAN CHARARA was born in Detroit in 1972, received his bachelor's degree from Wayne State University, and went on to earn a master's degree from New York University. His first book of poems, *Every Blessed Day*, is forthcoming from Hanging Loose Press. He has been published in many journals and anthologies and edits the literary publication, *Graffiti Rag*. A new book of poetry, *The Alchemist's Diary*, is forthcoming from Hanging Loose Press. Charara lives in New York City.

ESPERANZA M. CINTRON is a native Detroiter. Her poetry and short fiction have been published in a number of anthologies. She holds a doctorate in English literature from the State University of New York at Albany. "Street Market Requiem" is #5 in her New Detroit series, the post-Coleman era.

JAMES CLAY is a Detroit-area poet and short story writer published in area magazines and has released numerous books of his own over the past eight years. He has also been an active spoken word performer and has organized dozens of open-mic and performance shows throughout the past ten years. His new book of stories and prose is scheduled for release in the fall of 2001.

ANDREI CODRESCU emigrated from Romania to Detroit in time for the 1967 riots. His friends include John Sinclair, Jim Gustafson, Walter Hall, Ken Mikolowski, Bradley Jones, and other notable Detroiters.

WALTER COX has been published in past issues of Broadside Press anthologies. "Rosedale Street" was originally published in the *Broadside Series*.

STELLA CREWS is the author of two books, *Salad in August* and *Thieves or the Laundromat Bandit*. She coedited *HIPology* with Ron Allen for Broadside Press in 1990. For the last nine years, she has been writing science fiction novels.

ROBERT DANA's most recent books are *A Community of Writers: Paul Engle & The Iowa Writers' Workshop* (University of Iowa Press, 1999) and *Summer* (Anhinga Press, 2000), a new collection of poems. "Simple" first appeared in *The Iowa Review*.

JIM DANIELS was born in Detroit in 1956. He is the author of five collections of poetry, including *Blue Jesus* (Carnegie Mellon University Press, 2000), and one collection of stories, *No Pets* (Bottom Dog Press, 1999). "Hard Rock" is reprinted from *Punching Out* (Wayne State University Press, 1990). "Detroit Hymns, Christmas Eve" and "Time, Temperature" are reprinted from *M-80* (University of Pittsburgh Press, 1993).

TOI DERRICOTTE's latest books are *The Black Notebooks*, a memoir, and *Tender*. *The Black Notebooks* won the Annesfield Wolf Award in nonfiction and the nonfiction award from the Black Caucus of the American Library Association. *Tender* won the Paterson Poetry Prize. She is cofounder of CAVE CANEM, the historic workshop retreat for African American poets. Both poems are from *Captivity* (University of Pittsburgh Press).

MARK DONOVAN has lived in the Detroit area most of his life. He is currently a corporate slave for an automotive company, has a wife and three children, edited a magazine called *Howling Dog* for 13 issues, and continues to create and dream in relative suburban obscurity.

GLORIA DYC, associate professor at the University of New Mexico-Gallup, is finishing a novel set in Detroit titled *The Actress*. "Cargo of Grace" first appeared in Volume 6 of *The Spirit That Moves Us*.

HENRIETTA EPSTEIN is a graduate of Wayne State University, where she studied with W. D. Snodgrass and Edward Hirsch. She has lived in the Detroit area for most of her life, and was a founder and president of the Poetry Resource Center of Michigan. Her poems have appeared in *Moving Out*, *Windsor Review*, *Denver Quarterly*, *The Bridge*, and *Contemporary Michigan Poetry*. "Confession of the Rouge Park Killer" is from a chapbook, *The Necessary Pearl* (Red Hanrahan Press). "Wedding Photograph: Detroit, 1935," originally appeared in *Contemporary Michigan Poetry* (Wayne State University Press).

LINDA NEMEC FOSTER's poetry has been widely published in such journals as *The Georgia Review*, *Nimrod*, *River Styx*, and *Quarterly West*. She is the author of four books; the most recent title is the award-winning *Living in the Fire Nest*. Her new collection of poems, *Amber Necklace from Gdansk*, is forthcoming from Louisiana State University Press. "Detroit" first appeared in the *Midwest Poetry Review*. It was also included in the book *Living in the Fire Nest* (Ridgeway Press) and the anthology *Peninsula* (Michigan State University Press).

LARRY GABRIEL wrote his first poem at age twelve and hasn't looked back. He's editor of the *Metro Times*.

JOAN GARTLAND is a native of Brooklyn, New York. She has lived in Detroit since the sixties. Her poetry has been published in various magazines and anthologies, and her book, *A Passionate Distance*, was published by Ridgeway Press in 1991. "Song in Tender Black" first appeared in *Moving Out*, and "Egyptian Gallery in August" appears in *A Passionate Distance*.

JOSÉ GARZA is a longtime Southwest Detroit poet and artist. He has published several collections of his poetry and fiction over the years and has worked extensively with Detroit's Casa de Unidad Cultural Center.

DAN GEORGAKAS is coauthor of *Detroit: I Do Mind Dying* and *Solidarity Forever*. His poetry has appeared in anthologies such as *31 New American Poets* and *Advance Token to Boardwalk*. "October Song" originally appeared in *Three Red Stars*.

CHARLES A. GERVIN is a longtime Detroit poet now living and working in Washington, D.C. He is widely published, and was the cofounder of The Trobar Gallery in Detroit's Cass Corrdior in the 1980s.

MICHELE GIBBS' coming-of-age as an activist parallels the civil rights and student movements of the 1960s and the black power movement of the 1970s. Her contributions to African-American, women's, and workers' studies helped to lay the foundation for current efforts at academic diversification. While editor of *City Arts Quarterly*, the Detroit Common Council presented her with the 1987 Spirit of Detroit Award. Ms. Gibbs lives in Oaxaca, Mexico.

PERRI GIOVANNUCCI recently received the Alfred Boas prize of the Academy of American Poets.

MAURICE GREENIA, JR. was born October 20, 1953. He grew up in Detroit. By 1976, he started to make assemblages of his work to photocopy and distribute. He's shown his artwork in galleries and streets around Detroit and in France.

JIM GUSTAFSON's poems "The Idea of Detroit" and "Jukebox" were first published by The Alternative Press.

AURORA HARRIS is the program director of The World Voice Literary Series at The Graystone International Jazz Museum in Detroit. Her poems appear in *Brooding the Heartlands* (Bottom Dog Press, 1998) and other poetry journals.

BILL HARRIS is a Wayne State University English professor. His publications include *Riffs & Coda*, two dramas from Broadside Press, and two books of poems, *Yardbird Suite* (Michigan State University Press) and *Ringmaster's Array* (Past Tense Press).

KALEEMA HASAN has been writing and doing important community cultural work in Detroit for many years. She has also authored several books of poetry.

ROBERT HAYDEN (1913–1980) grew up in Detroit's Black Bottom and became one of Detroit's most famous poets. He is the author of several books of poetry, including *Heart-Shape in the Dust*, *The Lion and the Archer*, *Figures of Times: Poems*, *A Ballad of Remembrance*, *Selected Poems*, *Words in the Mourning Time*, *Night-Blooming Cereus*, *Angle of Ascent*, *American Journal*, and *Collected Poems*. He graduated from Wayne State University (then Detroit City College) and received an M.A.

in English from the University of Michigan, where he became professor of creative writing. He served as Poet-in-Residence at the Library of Congress (1976–1977).

ERROL A. HENDERSON is a former editor of the *Wayne Literary Review* and has performed his poetry throughout the United States. He is a long-time activist and is known for his community work with gang members and minority youth across the United States. He is a professor in the Department of Political Science at Wayne State University where he teaches international relations.

BARBARA HENNING's poetry collections include *Smoking in the Twilight Bar* and *Love Makes Thinking Dark* (United Artists). A novel, *Black Lace*, and a new collection of poems, *Detective Sentences*, are forthcoming from Spuyten Duyvil. Pamphlets include *Me and My Dog* (Poetry New York), *In Between* (Spectacular Diseases), and *The Passion of Signs* (Leave Books). "As A Corrective" originally appeared in *K(Satchel)* as a section of the poem "Detective Sentences."

LOLITA HERNANDEZ is currently writing short fiction. "Quiet Battles" was originally published by Wayne State University Press, and "Garcia's Market" by Ridgeway Press.

JERRY HERRON is professor of English and director of the American Studies Program at Wayne State University in Detroit. His publications include *Universities and the Myth of Cultural Decline* and *AfterCulture: Detroit and the Humiliation of History*.

ELLEN HILDRETH writes and performs her work in the shadow of the Heidelberg Project. John Sinclair has said of her poetry, "what a wonderful treat to read."

EDWARD HIRSCH has published five books of poems, including *Earthly Measures* and *On Love*, and two books of prose, *How to Read a Poem* and *Fall in Love with Poetry and Responsive Reading*. He has taught at Wayne State University and the University of Houston. "Three Journeys" originally appeared in *Wild Gratitude* from Alfred A. Knopf (1986).

ANN HOLDREITH is a multidimensional artist who combines her talents as a writer, vocalist, dancer, and actress in her performance art. She is a 1999 Pushcart Prize nominee. Her publishing credits include Plainview Press, Aether, Snakeskin, and Poetry Motel. Ann teaches poetry and performance for the Writer's Voice.

DAN HUGHES is professor emeritus at Wayne State University and author of several collections of poems including *You Are Not Stendhal: New and Selected Poems, Falling,* and *Spirit Traps.*

KIM HUNTER is a lifelong Detroiter and a media producer whose poetry has appeared in *Graffiti Rag, Dispatch, Against the Current,* and many other publications. He has also conducted many poetry workshops for youth and adjudicated competitions.

CLARK IVERSON is a poet and writer who teaches English part-time in the Detroit area. He is married and has two children.

MURRAY JACKSON is founding president of Wayne County Community College, professor emeritus of higher education at the University of Michigan, and a member of the Board of Governors at Wayne State University. "Dudley Randall" and "8 Ball in Side Pocket" first appeared in *Watermelon Rinds and Cherry Pits, Poems by Murray Jackson* (Broadside Press, 1991).

GEOFFREY JACQUES is the author of two collections of poems: *Hunger and Other Poems* (Ridgeway, 1993) and *Suspended Knowledge* (Adastra, 1998). His essays and articles have appeared in numerous periodicals, including *NKA Journal of Contemporary African Art, Publishers Weekly, Black Issues Book Review, Cineaste,* and the Detroit *Metro Times.* His essay, "Listening to Jazz," appears in *American Popular Music: New Approaches to the Twentieth Century,* Rachel Rubin and Jeffrey Melnick, eds. (University of Massachusetts Press, 1996). Born in Detroit, he lives in Brooklyn, NY. "Giant" and "The Blab of the Pave" are from the author's manuscript.

STEPHEN JONES is a poet, teacher, and journalist. He lives in Detroit with his wife, Colette Gilewicz, and their son, Alexander Jones.

LAWRENCE JOSEPH was born in Detroit in 1948. He is the author of three books of poems, *Before Our Eyes* (Farrar, Straus & Giroux, 1993), *Curriculum Vitae* (University of Pittsburgh Press, 1988), and *Shouting at No One* (University of Pittsburgh Press, 1983). He is also the author of *Lawyerland,* a book of prose published by Farrar, Straus & Giroux in 1997. A Professor of Law at St John's University School of Law, he lives in New York City. "Curriculum Vitae" originally appeared in his book *Curriculum Vitae* (University of Pittsburgh Press).

NUBIA KAI is a native of Detroit, and received her B.A. and M.A. from Wayne State University. Poet, fiction writer, and playwright, she is the recipient of three Tompkins Awards, and a McCree Theater Award. She has received grants from the NEA and Michigan Council for the Arts. "Joe Louis" is from *Solos* (Lotus Press, 1988).

ANEB KGOSITSILE (Gloria House), educator, poet, and community activist, retired in 1998 from Wayne State University after 27 years as a professor of humanities. She earned a bachelor's and master's degree at the University of California, Berkeley, in French and Comparative Literature respectively. Her doctorate was completed in American Culture/History at the University of Michigan, where she was a CEW Scholar, and recipient of a Rackham Fellowship. Dr. House's publications include two poetry collections from Broadside Press, *Blood River* (1983) and *Rainrituals* (1990), as well as a book of sociopolitical commentary on the uses of environment in the United States, *Tower and Dungeon: A Study of Place and Power in America* (1991). Dr. House was named professor emerita at Wayne State in 1998.

FAYE KICKNOSWAY lives in Honolulu, a suburb of Detroit.

MARGO LAGATTUTA is a longtime Detroit area poet and editor. Her recent collections of poetry include *Embracing the Fall*, *NoEdgeLines*, and *Dream Givers*. She has edited several anthologies for Texas' Plain View Press. In addition, she is the weekly host of a Detroit area poetry radio program.

OLIVER LAGRONE's (1906–1995) poems are from *Dawnfire* (Lotus Press, 1989). Reprinted by permission of the publisher.

CHRISTINE LAHEY is a native Detroiter who has received the Avery Hopwood Award for Poetry from the University of Michigan and a Creative Artists Grant from the Michigan Council for the Arts. In 1983 she coedited the *Planet Detroit Anthology of Urban Poetry* with Kurt Nimmo. Christine teaches at College for Creative Studies (CCS) in Detroit where she specializes in interdisciplinary studies. "Motor City Men" appeared in *Sticks and Stones* (Urban Despair Chapbooks, 1980) and "Afterglow" in *All's Normal Here: A Charles Bukowski Primer*, ed. Loss Glazier (Ruddy Duck Press, 1985).

MICHAEL LAUCHLAN is a longtime Detroit poet and activist. He currently teaches at the University of Detroit Jesuit High School. His most recent book is *Sudden Parade* (Ridgeway Press).

JANET LAWLESS is a former student of Wayne State University and former resident of Hamtramck, Michigan. She was active in the Detroit literary community, publishing, editing literary journals, and helping to organize readings around the city. She moved to Seattle in 1997, and writes and reads in Seattle, but misses her hometown tremendously. "Fallen" has also appeared in *The Hamtramck Diaries*, published by The Wayne Writers' Forum.

PHILIP LEVINE was born in Detroit in 1928. He attended Central High School and Wayne State University where he received a B.A. (1950) and an M.A. (1955) in English. His most recent book is *The Mercy* (Knopf).

M. L. LIEBLER is the author of ten books of poetry including the recent *New & Selected from The Los Angeles Poets Collective* and *Breaking the Voodoo* (Adastra Press). He is the founding director of The YMCA National Writer's Voice Project in Detroit, and a faculty member at Wayne State University since 1980.

NAOMI LONG MADGETT, named poet laureate of Detroit in 2001, is the author of eight collections of poetry, beginning in 1941 and including the award-winning *Octavia and Other Poems* (Third World Press, 1988) and *Remembrances of Spring: Collected Early Poems* (Michigan State University Press, 1993). She is publisher/editor of Lotus Press and professor of English emeritus at Eastern Michigan University. "Grand Circus Park" is from *Pink Ladies in the Afternoon* (1972, 1990), and "City Nights" and "Good News" are from *Exits and Entrances* (1978), both by Naomi Long Madgett.

MIKE MADIAS is a chronicler of urban legends. His on-line magazine, *Detroit Hard Ball*, is a journal of social commentary that enjoys an international audience.

PETER MARKUS is a longtime Detroit poet and fiction writer. He teaches high school writing workshops for Terry Blackhawk's InsideOut program in Detroit Public Schools, and he is the author of *Still Lives with Whiskey Bottle*.

MARC MAURUS is a survivor of Vietnam and a closed-head injury. He has overcome all obstacles on his way to becoming a poet. The first Caucasian member of The Detroit Black Writer's Guild, a Plymouth Poet, and the host of the live venue, Poetry in Motion, he is a living example of the triumph of the human spirit. "5/8 Time" has been published in *Cokefish* and *Used Books*, the author's second collection from Gravity Presses.

JUDITH MCCOMBS is a poet and scholar whose creative books include *Sisters and Other Selves* (Glass Bell), *Against Nature: Wilderness Poems* (Dustbooks), and *Territories* (Mayapple). "In Praise of the Natural Flowing" appeared originally in *Poetry* 127, no. 4 (Jan. 1976), 207.

RAYMOND P. MCKINNEY, a member of the popular Detroit-bred "Musical McKinney Family" and an upright Bassist and classical cellist, is also known for his insightful poetry and tongue-twisting "Baffle-Gab." Ray, a recent transplant recipient, is currently exploring and enjoying his "second chance" at life.

KEN MIKOLOWSKI is editor, publisher, and printer of The Alternative Press. He is a Wayne State University graduate and member of the Cass Corridor Gang. Currently he is teaching poetry writing at the University of Michigan's Residential College in Ann Arbor. "January in Detroit" first appeared in his book *Thank you Call Again* from The Perishable Press. "Homage to Frank O'Hara" first appeared in his book *Big Enigmas* from Past Tents Press.

DEREK P. MILLER is a poet who lives and works in the Detroit area.

MARY MINOCK is the author of one book of poetry, *Love in the Upstairs Flat* (Mellen Poetry Press). She earns her living as an academic writer and teacher of rhetoric, and holds a doctorate in English from the University of Michigan. She is currently teaching at Madonna University and gathering poems for her second book of poetry, provisionally titled *The Tenants*. She lives in the same house where she grew up in Southwest Detroit. Mary Minock's "Down by the Boulevard Dock" and "The Wildflowers of Detroit" both originally appeared in *Love in the Upstairs Flat* (Mellen Poetry Press, 1995).

CHRISTINE MONHOLLEN is editor of *DISPATCH Detroit*, an ongoing poetry, prose, and art project. She has published two books of poetry, *Razor Moon* (Triage Press, 1992) and *Accessory* (1995). Monhollen's next book of poetry, *Near Absence of Pink*, is due for release in 2002.

WARDELL MONTGOMERY, JR. performs humorous and serious poetry with pizzazz! He's an easy to understand urban folk poet whose award-winning work has been praised by educators and just plain folk in Detroit, New York, and Denver. "Roses are Red" originally appeared in his chapbook, *Let's Not Go There.*

JESSICA CARE MOORE-SIMMONS is a writer, poet, performance artist, and book publisher from Detroit, currently based in Atlanta, GA. She has performed across the U.S. and abroad and has been widely anthologized. The CEO of Moore Black Press and co-owner of MoorEpics: the Poetry Planet, Care Moore is the author of *The Words Don't Fit in My Mouth* and *The Alphabet Verses the Ghetto,* and publisher of Saul Williams' *The Seventh Octave* and Sharrif Simmons' *Fast Cities and Objects That Burn.* She is currently editing MBP's first anthology, *The Poetry of Emcees.* She is the author of three plays and has a live CD with her poetry-rock band, Detroit Read (pronounced like the color). She's also an Apollo Legend. "Black Coals with Diamond Hearts" appears courtesy of Moore Black Press.

JAN MORDENSKI is a westsider, born and raised in Detroit back in the days of Mayor Miriani. She taught creative writing in the Detroit area for more than 25 years. Her work has been published in the U.S., as well as in the other former colonies. She still has her first fielder's mitt. "In the Sixties . . ." was first published in *The Bridge.*

EDWARD MORIN is a well-known Detroit poet and college teacher now living and writing in Ann Arbor. He has published several books, including the recent *Labor Day at Walden Pond* (Ridgeway Press).

TED NAGY is a graduate of Wayne State University and is currently working for the Ford Detroit International Jazz Festival in the Artist Relations Department. He composes and teaches music around the Detroit area.

SCHAARAZETTA NATELEGE is a graduate of the University of Michigan, where she was a student of Robert Hayden. Her poetry has been published in *Solid Ground, Obsidian, The South End,* and *Promenade.*

DAVID J. NELSON is a former Detroit poet and cofounder of the internationally known performance poetry ensemble, The Last Poets. His poetry appears on CDs and records dating back to the late 1960s. He is currently living and working in the arts community in St. Louis.

KRISTIN PALM is a freelance journalist and, through InsideOut, Inc., a writer-in-residence in the Detroit Public Schools. She lives in Detroit, where she is completing a graduate degree in urban planning at Wayne State University. "Motor City Trilogy" appeared in the anthology *Up from the Soles of Our Feet*, published by Plain View Press.

TED PEARSON, a native Californian, moved to Detroit in 1997. He is the author of 15 books of poetry and currently teaches composition and creative writing at Wayne State University. Selections from "The Blue Table" and from Coulomb's Law" are excerpted from EVIDENCE: 1975–1989 (Gaz, 1989).

SARAH JEANNE PETERS has an M.A. in English literature from Wayne State University and has taught English at a variety of schools in the Detroit area. She has lived in the heart of Detroit for nine years and is currently the senior editor at detroit.citysearch.com, an arts and entertainment city guide. This is the first publishing of "First Light."

TOM PETERS, JR. was born on the corner of 7 Mile and Mack in 1960. His best memories of Detroit were watching the riots and the 1968 Tigers (Bill Freehan, #11, was his first autograph). "Ode to a '64 Chrysler" first appeared in *Camp Kerouac, Bombay Gin*, and in *Over the Roofs of the World* (Cityful Press).

T. R. PETERS, SR. wrote the novel *Two Weeks in the Forties* and *Into the Emerald City with Gangster Sunglasses*, a collection of stories, poems, and essays. His work has been included in *Third Coast: Contemporary Michigan Fiction* (Wayne State University Press), and has won the Hillsdale College Literary Award. "Ghosts of the Central Area: Detroit" appeared in *Into the Emerald City with Gangster Sunglasses*.

LAWRENCE PIKE (1932–1995) was one of Detroit's original voices in the 1960s and beyond. He authored several collections of poetry and fiction, including *Pierced By Sound* (Ridgeway Press), his last publication before his untimely death in 1995. He was writer-in-residence at Macomb Community College for over thirty years.

AARON IBIN PORI PITTS is a Detroit-based multi-media performance poet, filmmaker, and printmaker. He graduated with a B.F.A. in printmaking and film communications from Wayne State University. He is a cofounder and past president of the Michigan Chapter of the National Conference of Artists. He has received three regional artist project grants from the National Endowment for the Arts and has completed several public art installations for the "Ogun" project. His most recent exhibit, at the Charles H. Wright Museum of African American History, included "Abandoned Automobile," which appears on the cover of this volume.

SONYA MARIE POUNCY was born and raised in Detroit. She received her baccalaureate in mechanical engineering from Purdue University. She currently works as an engineer and poet in the city of Detroit.

DUDLEY RANDALL (1914–2000) was the first poet laureate of Detroit (1981–2000) and the author of six books of poetry: *Poem Counterpoem* (with Margaret Danner), *Cities Burning, After the Killing, More to Remember, Love You,* and *A Litany of Friends.* He was the founding editor/publisher of Broadside Press, and the editor of numerous anthologies of black poetry. His poetry has been translated into many languages, including Russian. "Old Witherington" and "Bag Woman" appeared in *A Litany of Friends* (Lotus Press, 1981). "George" appeared in *Poem Counterpoem* (1966).

JON RANDALL is a native Detroiter and the nephew of Dudley Randall. He published his first book of poetry, *Indigoes,* at Broadside Press during the Black Arts Movement. He currently lives and works in Chicago.

KEVIN RASHID is a poet and lifetime Detroit resident. He teaches evening classes in creative writing and composition at Marygrove College and Wayne State University, where he is also a full-time groundskeeper.

MARILYNN RASHID's poems, essays, and translations have appeared in various publications. She is a lecturer in Spanish at Wayne State University.

EUGENE B. REDMOND is professor of English and chair of the Creative Writing Committee at Southern Illinois University–Edwardsville. He currently serves as poet laureate of East St. Louis, a post to which he was appointed in 1976, and founding editor of *Drumvoices Revue.* He won the American Book Award in 1993 for *The Eye in the Ceiling.* "Aerolingual Poet of Prey" is reprinted from *Drumvoices Revue.* "Detroit Circa 1989/90" is from an unpublished manuscript by the author. He was a professor at Wayne State University during the 1980s and returns often to read his poetry and to participate in cultural activities in Detroit.

JOHN R. REED is professor of English at Wayne State University. He has had four books of poems published, the most recent being *Life Sentences* (1996).

LESLIE REESE is a poet and educator specializing in helping young people to affirm themselves and their experiences through language. She is the author of *Upside Down Tapestry Mosaic History* (Broadside Press) and a graduate of Alabama A & M University. Her work has appeared in the anthologies *The Spirit In the Word, More Light, The Black Woman's Gumbo Ya-Ya, Adam of Ife, HIPology,* and *Nostalgia For The Present,* as well as in the journals *SEEDS, Obsidian II, Michigan Quarterly Review,* and *Solid Ground.* "I Love You (The Heidelberg Project)" was originally published in *Drumvoices Revue.*

ROD REINHART heads the Plymouth Poets and has been appointed as poet-in-residence for Plymouth, MI. He is author of *Spiritual Aerobics for the 21st Century.* "I am Waiting" was published in *History's Mill* in 1982.

JUDITH ROCHE was born and raised in Detroit, though she now lives in Seattle. She has published two collections of poetry and won a 1999 American Book Award for coediting *First Fish, First People, Salmon Tales of the North Pacific Rim* (University of Washington Press), a collection about wild salmon. "Serious Childhood" was originally published in *Ghosts* (Empty Bowl Press, 1984).

MICHELE VALERIE RONNICK is associate professor in Wayne State University's Department of Classics, Greek, and Latin. She is the author of 96 articles and notes in refereed journals. Her research interests include Latin literature, neo-Latin, and the classical tradition.

IRENE ROSEMOND is a published poet and author. She was raised in upstate New York and began writing at a very young age. Irene is the author of the book *Reflections,* published by Broadside Press of Detroit. She is also a poet-in-residence for the Detroit Public Library system.

MICHAEL ASHTON ROSEMOND is a published poet and author. His latest book of poetry is a volume of poems entitled *This Is My Love.* He is currently writing a mystery novel about Detroit entitled *Murder in Babylon.*

JOHN RYBICKI's stories and poems have appeared in the *North American Review, Field, Ohio Review, Quarterly West, Bomb,* and others. He grew up on Detroit's eastside, and currently teaches creative writing at Pelham Middle School—near the shadow of old Tiger Stadium. He is the author of *Traveling at High Speeds* (New Issues Poetry Press).

OSVALDO R. SABINO was born in Caseros, Provincia de Buenos Aires, Argentina in 1951, and emigrated to the U.S. in 1979. He became an American citizen in 1984. After earning his M.A. in 1987 from University of California-San Diego, Sabino earned his doctorate from Boston University in 1993. He's had many books published, including *Borges; Atlantida; La historia de las panteras y de algunos de los animales conversos; El juegete erotico; Jorge Luis Borges: Una nueva vision de "Ulrica"* (1999); and *Nadando en el volcan* (forthcoming). James Hoggard's translation of "Chameleon Posing with a Passport" originally appeared in *Clackamas Literary Review.* The poem appears in its original Spanish version in the volume *Mujeres Solas.* He currently lives in Detroit and has taught writing at Wayne State University.

JACQUELINE RAE RAWLSON SANCHEZ has been a published poet since 1975. In 1983 she became the owner/publisher/editor of *The Sounds of Poetry* (magazines & chapbooks). In that same year, she founded The Latino Poets' Association and is currently CEO and director. This is the first publishing of "Drew's Mom."

TRINIDAD SÁNCHEZ, JR. is a Detroit poet whose poetry is rooted in the latino urban experience. He is the author of several books of poetry, including *Why Am I So Brown?* and has won numerous awards. When not traveling around the country lecturing and reciting his poetry, he works at Family Star Early Head Start as community outreach coordinator in Denver, Colorado.

STEVEN SCHREINER is the author of *Too Soon to Leave* (Ridgeway Press, 1997). His recent poems have appeared in *Colorado Review, Image,* and *River Styx.* He studied at Wayne State University and is associate professor of English at University of Missouri–St. Louis. "Passion Fruit" originally appeared in *HIPology.*

DENISE SEDMAN was born and raised in Detroit until her family moved to the suburbs when she was twelve years old. She has a B.A. from Oakland University and has had a variety of poems, fiction, and essays published. She now lives in Royal Oak, but still considers herself a "salty girl from Detroit City."

SEMAJ has published *The Dancing Shoes on Fire Book of Poetry,* and is director of Muhammad University of Islam in Detroit. She reads with a full band, mixing funk, fusion, classic, and hip-hop. She has performed at a wide variety of venues, including off-Broadway, and was chosen by Detroit's *Metro Times* as one (of twenty) of "Detroit's Finest."

DENNIS SHEA has been a Detroit resident for twenty-five years. He works as a proofreader and writer for Detroit's *Metro Times*. His cynicism and humor mask an unwavering idealism.

JOHN SINCLAIR is a nationally known and widely respected jazz and blues poet. He cofounded, with George Tysh, the legendary Detroit Artist Workshop in the Cass Corrdior during the early 1960s. His books include *We Just Change the Beat* (Ridgeway Press) and *Guitar Army*. Much of his work with music and poetry appears on several nationally released CDs. He currently lives and writes in New Orleans with his wife, Penny.

ELLA SINGER is program coordinator for the Youth Urban Agenda/Civic Literacy Project at Wayne State University. In addition she is a spoken word performer, visual artist, and coach for Detroit's 1999 SLAM Poetry Team.

W. D. SNODGRASS is a distinguished professor emeritus at the University of Delaware and was a professor of English at Wayne State University from 1959–67. He lives with wife, Kathleen, in Erieville, NY and San Miguel de Allende, Mexico. "Old Apple Trees" appeared in *If Birds Build with Your Hair* (Madja Press, 1979) and was reprinted in *Selected Poems, 1957–1987* (Soho Press, 1987).

ELIZABETH ANNE SOCOLOW was a Detroit poet from New Jersey until July 1999, when she became a New Jersey poet from Detroit. She has lived in the area and taught at the Writer's Voice, Wayne State University, Lawrence Technological University, University of Michigan/Dearborn, and Oakland Community College for some eight years in various combinations.

KEITH CARTER STERLING is a Detroit area writer and artist who is the author of two poetry collections, *Rendezvous* and *The Water Bearers*.

RENÉE TAMBEAU is a Detroit area actress, poet, and writer. She is a founding member of the poetry band *Spoke*. A version of *Renaissance* can be heard on their second CD, *Sw'elegant*.

TERESA TAN is a vibrational poet and author of *Intangible: A Book of Poetry*. Her work explores the mystery and the dance of infinite intelligence in worlds seen and unseen. "I will never understand the city" first appeared in the *Metro Times'* summer fiction edition.

KEITH TAYLOR has published five chapbooks of poetry and one collection of very short stories. In 2000 he coedited *The Huron River: Voices from the Watershed*, an anthology published by the University of Michigan Press. "Detroit Dancing" first appeared in the literary journal *Notus*. It was reprinted in *Everything I Need* (March Street Press, 1996).

DENNIS TEICHMAN is the editor of Past Tents Press. He is a graduate of Wayne State University. His books of poetry include *Edge to Edge* and *V8*.

STEPHEN TUDOR (1933–1994) was a sailor and poet who lived in Detroit on the water—just minutes from Lake St. Clair and the Detroit River. Consequently, when he wrote about Detroit, he showed it to us from the water—Detroit as the gateway to the Great Lakes. "Factories Along the River" and "Detroit River North to South" were both published in *Hangdog Reef: Poems Sailing the Great Lakes* (Wayne State University Press, 1989) and in *Haul-Out* (Wayne State University Press, 1996).

CHRIS TYSH teaches creative writing and women's studies at Wayne State University. Her latest publications include *Coat of Arms, In the Name*, and *Continuity Girl*. Scenes 6 and 7 are from her play in verse, *Car Men, a play in d*, published in *In the Name* (Past Tents Press, 1994). *Car Men, a play in d* was premiered at The Detroit Institute of Arts, November 15, 1996.

GEORGE TYSH is arts editor for the *Metro Times*. His latest book of poems, *Dream Sites: A Visual Essay*, is from Past Tents Press/Cranbrook Art Museum. "Aire" and "Babes" were first published in *Echolalia* (New York: United Artists Books, 1992).

MELANIE VAN DER TUIN has been a Detroit-area poet since the age of ten. More recently, she earned her M.A. in English from Wayne State University under the guidance of mentors Anca Vlasopolos and M. L. Liebler. Melanie now lives in Ferndale with her cat, Pagan, who is waiting for her to make it "big" so that he can upgrade to Fancy Feast.

HILDA VEST is a previous editor/publisher of Broadside Press. She has won the Detroit Women Writers Poetry Award. The two poems published here originally appeared in *Sorrow's End*, a collection by the author.

ANCA VLASOPOLOS has published a poetry collection, *Through the Straits, At Large*, a chapbook, *The Evidence of Spring*, a detective novel, *Missing Members*, over a hundred poems in literary magazines, and most recently *No Return Address: A Memoir of Displacement* (New York: Columbia University Press, 2000). She also has written a libretto for an opera performed by the Hilberry Theatre and the Michigan Opera Theatre. "March of Dimes, April in Detroit" appeared in her collection *Through the Straits, At Large* (Ridgeway Press, 1998).

RAYFIELD WALLER is a graduate of the Wayne State University English Department (where he won 14 Tompkins and Bruenton prizes for poetry, fiction, and essay), a past editor of the *Wayne Review*, and a former student of Alvin Aubert. An eastside Detroit native, he holds graduate degrees from Cornell, where he studied with poet Phyllis Janowitz and Nobel playwright Wole Soyinka. He has two book of poems, *Abstract Blues* (Broadside, 1987) and *Television Funereal* (Exit-Stencial, 1999), has traveled widely in Afrika and Europe, and participated in the University of Paris "American Jazz Poets" readings in 1991. He currently teaches at Florida International University and is working on a novel and a screenplay.

DAVID WATSON is a lifelong Detroit resident. He has published essays, journalism, and poetry in a variety of publications. His third book of essays, *Against the Megamachine* (Autonomedia) was published in 1998. "Trust Jesus" originally appeared in *DISPATCH Detroit* (1998).

BARRETT WATTEN is a founding member of the Language School of poetry. He emigrated from the San Francisco Bay Area to Detroit in 1994. Presently he is associate professor of English at Wayne State University, where he teaches modernism and cultural studies. His books include a collected poems anthology, *Frame: 1971–1990* (Sun & Moon Press, 1997), and *Bad History* (Atelos, 1998). He was editor of *This* magazine and This Press in the 1970s and 1980s. He was also coeditor, with Lyn Hejinian, of *Poetics Journal* from 1982 to 1998. "Tibet" was originally published in *Opera — Works* (Big Sky Books, 1975), and is reprinted from *Frame: 1971–1990*. The selection from *Under Erasure* is reprinted from *Under Erasure* (Zasterle Press, 1991).

KIM WEBB writes and paints in Hamtramck, MI where he has been an active organizer. Poems from his book *Abstract Cores* (Ridgeway Press, 1996) were nominated for a Pushcart Prize. He has an M.F.A. from the University of Tennessee (1983).

MARY ANN WEHLER began writing at 60. Her book *Walking Through Deep Snow* was published in 1997. She is assistant to the director of the Writer's Voice, and editor of the newsletter. "They Walked a Mile for a Camel, the Man's cigarette" was first published in *Variations on the Ordinary* (Plain View Press, 1995), an anthology, and in *Walking through Deep Snow.*

KAREN WILLIAMS, a Cave Canem Fellow, is a member of the Detroit Writer's Voice and chair of the Detroit Writer's Guild. Her poetry and fiction have been published widely.

TYRONE WILLIAMS teaches English literature at Xavier University in Cincinnati, OH. His chapbook, *Convalescence*, was published by Ridgeway Press.

WILLIE WILLIAMS was born Black by the Detroit River in the year Willie Mays grew into a giant. As a child of the 1960s, he will never lose his idealism or voice in the struggle for freedom with his words as weapons.